UNDERSTANDING

JOHN GARDNER

Understanding Contemporary
American Literature

Matthew J. Bruccoli, Editor

UNDERSTANDING
John
GARDNER

JOHN M. HOWELL

UNIVERSITY OF SOUTH CAROLINA PRESS

For Sue and Evan

Copyright © 1993 University of South Carolina

130605.

Published in Columbia, South Carolina, by the
University of South Carolina Press

Manufactured in the United States of America

Library of Congress Cataloging-in-Publication Data

Howell, John Michael, 1933–
    Understanding John Gardner / by John M. Howell.
        p.   cm. — (Understanding contemporary American literature)
    Includes bibliographical references and index.
    ISBN 0–87249–872–7 (acid-free paper)
    1. Gardner, John, 1933–   —Criticism and interpretation.
    I. Title.   II. Series.
    PS3557.A712Z69   1993
    813'.54—dc20   93–9892

CONTENTS

Understanding Contemporary American Literature has been planned as a series of guides or companions for students as well as good nonacademic readers. The editor and publisher perceive a need for these volumes because much of the influential contemporary literature makes special demands. Uninitiated readers encounter difficulty in approaching works that depart from the traditional forms and techniques of prose and poetry. Literature relies on conventions, but the conventions keep evolving; new writers form their own conventions—which in time may become familiar. Put simply, *UCAL* provides instruction in how to read certain contemporary writers—identifying and explicating their material, themes, use of language, point of view, structures, symbolism, and responses to experience.

The word *understanding* in the series title was deliberately chosen. Many willing readers lack an adequate understanding of how contemporary literature works; that is, what the author is attempting to express and the means by which it is conveyed. Although the criticism and analysis in the series have been aimed at a level of general accessibility, these introductory volumes are meant to be applied in conjunction with the works they cover. Thus they do not provide a substitute for the works and authors they introduce, but rather prepare the reader for more profitable literary experiences.

M. J. B.

ACKNOWLEDGMENTS

Special thanks to Richard F. Peterson, Professor and Chair of English, who encouraged my research and offered editorial advice; and to my wife, Sue Howell, who influenced and tempered the writing of this book from start to finish.

UNDERSTANDING
JOHN GARDNER

CHAPTER ONE

Understanding John Gardner

Career

John Gardner's death in a motorcycle accident near Susquehanna, Pennsylvania, on 14 September 1982, stilled a vital force in American literature. He was a prolific author and an inspiring teacher and editor. Three of his novels—*The Sunlight Dialogues* (1972), *Nickel Mountain* (1973), and *October Light* (1976)—became best-sellers at the time of publication; and *Grendel* (1971), ultimately his most popular novel, is widely taught in American colleges and high schools.

John Champlin Gardner, Jr. was born in Batavia, New York, on 21 July 1933, the eldest of four children. His father was a dairyman and a lay preacher in the Presbyterian church; his mother was an English teacher in the local schools.

Gardner graduated from the Batavia high school, and attended DePauw University for two years. In 1953 he married Joan Louise Patterson and transferred to Washington University in St. Louis. Upon graduation from Washington University (Phi Beta Kappa) in 1955, he used a Woodrow Wilson Fellowship to attend the University of Iowa, where he participated in the writing workshops, studied Anglo-Saxon and medieval literature, and submitted a novel, ''The Old Men,'' as his doctoral dissertation in 1958.

After receiving his Ph.D., Gardner taught briefly at Oberlin College, Chico State College, and San Francisco State College. In September 1965 he became an associate professor of English at Southern Illinois University-Carbondale, where he regularly taught Anglo-Saxon and medieval studies until September 1974. Here, in addition to writing fiction and poetry, he wrote and edited scholarly books for the Southern Illinois University Press. After brief stints at Bennington College, Williams College, Skidmore College, and George Mason University, he joined the faculty of the State University of New York at Binghamton in 1978, where he was teaching in the creative writing program at the time of his death.

Though the publication of Gardner's first novel, *The Resurrection* (1966), was barely noticed, *The Wreckage of Agathon* (1970) received mixed reviews in important newspapers and magazines. It was *Grendel* (1971), however, which brought him national recognition. Richard Locke of the *New York Times* called Gardner "a major contemporary writer,"[1] and the other reviewers were almost as enthusiastic.[2] Though there was less unanimity about *The Sunlight Dialogues* (1972), there were nevertheless many enthusiastic and perceptive responses, and the novel remained on the *New York Times* bestsellers list for fifteen weeks. But then, his career seemingly well-launched, Gardner wrote *Jason and Medeia* (1973)—an imitation in "sprung hexameters" of a classical epic, which most reviewers greeted with bewilderment and dismay, and some with outright hostility.

Within the year, however, Gardner was back on the bestsellers lists with *Nickel Mountain: A Pastoral Novel* (1973)—an episodic work fashioned from eight closely related short stories written between 1954 and 1965. Unfamiliar with the novel's genesis, some reviewers assumed enthusiastically that Gardner had given up his technical innovations and philosophical speculations and returned to simpler narratives and themes. They were surprised, therefore, when Gardner continued in the direction that *Grendel* had pointed, exploring the techniques of "metafiction" (fiction about fiction) in *The King's Indian: Stories and Tales* (1974), a virtuoso performance which received extremes of praise and denigration.

Gardner did in fact return to a conventional narrative with the autobiographical novel "Stillness," which he drafted in spring, 1975, shortly after moving to Bennington, Vermont. But he soon abandoned that novel (published posthumously in 1986) to write *October Light* (1976), a record of the tragicomic battle of an elderly brother and his older sister who, isolated in her bedroom, reads and reacts to fragments from a comic novel, *The Smugglers of Lost Souls' Rock*. Though some reviewers faulted *October Light* for its "double" narrative, it received the National Book Critics Circle Award for outstanding fiction in 1976, and it became, like *The Sunlight Dialogues* and *Nickel Mountain,* a best-seller.

October Light was Gardner's last major success. In 1977, distracted by personal, financial, and professional crises, he began to lose control over his art. He entered into prolonged divorce litigation with his wife; he was operated on for colonic cancer; and he faced mounting liabilities for unpaid taxes. But impinging even more directly upon his career was the publication in 1977 of *The Poetry of Chaucer* and *The Life & Times of Chaucer,* which damaged his reputation as a scholar-critic. Journalistic book reviewers focused largely on the biography, finding it entertaining and useful, but the academic reviewers generally faulted Gardner for whimsical interpretations and unreliable scholarship in both books.[3]

A similar pattern of response greeted Gardner's "literary manifesto," *On Moral Fiction* (1978). At first there was general enthusiasm in the popular media, and Gardner's polemic on the state of contemporary fiction received more reviews than any of his best-selling novels. Journalists praised his assertion that fiction should search for "truths to live by," and some of them mistakenly assumed he was asking for representational, or "realistic," fiction. Many academic critics were also enthusiastic, and used Gardner's manifesto to interpret his fiction. Ultimately, however, *On Moral Fiction* presented a distorted view of the practice, if not the purpose, of Gardner's own fiction, and hurt his career. Though the book offered many illuminating insights into the nature and potential of fiction, readers were irritated by Gardner's harsh and deliberately provocative judgments of his contemporaries. Ultimately, despite much early enthusiasm, the critical response was negative, and this negative response influenced the often hostile reviews of Gardner's later (and generally weaker) fiction: *Freddy's Book* (1980), *The Art of Living and Other Stories* (1981), *Mickelsson's Ghosts* (1982), and even Nicholas Delbanco's posthumous edition of the unfinished novels *"Stillness" and "Shadows"* (1986).

At the time of his death, Gardner had just finished a translation, with John Maier, of the epic *Gilgamesh* (1984). But more critically and biographically significant was his completion of two books devoted to the process of fiction: *On Becoming a Novelist* (1983), a look at the life and goals of a writer, including an autobiographical perspective on his own writing; and *The Art of Fiction: Notes on Craft for Young Writers* (1984), a guide now widely used in college classes.

Overview

Gardner saw his central characters as "clowns," imitation human beings with heads full of straw. When the clown tries and fails to imitate the acrobat—the complete human being in Gardner's metaphorical circus—he becomes self-conscious and inhibited, thus further removed from the emotional affirmation which leads to a transcendence of the self and a "connectedness" with humanity. If, through an act of selfless love or compassion, the clown reaches out to humanity and life, he will experience an earthbound—as opposed to a metaphysical—version of what Gardner's favorite hymn calls "Amazing Grace." But if, on the other hand, the clown lapses into total self-consciousness and accepts the kind of "perverse rationality"[4] that Gardner equated with Jean-Paul Sartre's existentialism, then he risks falling into nihilism—and to Gardner, nihilists are "monsters" who have given up the battle for faith over despair.

Gardner generally portrays his "clowns" and other characters with cartoonlike images that suggest, by abstraction and metaphorical action, their resemblance to animals: a bear, an owl, a mole, a chicken. Though he wanted depth of characterization in his work, he also wanted to avoid sentimentality, and he tried to gain distance by portraying his characters as grotesques—or "cartoons"—as well as human beings. Thus his characters, like those of William Faulkner, or Flannery O'Connor, or Charles Dickens, are often slightly distorted in their physical features, and, as noted, often compared to animals. But Gardner sometimes goes beyond the "cartoons" that he enjoyed in these and other essentially Gothic writers to represent events which can only be seen in animated cartoons—or perhaps in the "magic realism" of Latin American writers like Gabriel Garcia Marquez. (Gardner's novel *October Light* indicates, for example, that when James Page blasted his sister's TV set with a shotgun, she "had shot up three feet into the air and fainted dead away and gone blue all over. . . .")[5]

Gardner read and reread Dickens's novels as an adolescent. He was fascinated with the grotesque characters and with the way Dickens's narratives developed in counterpoint to the visual abstractions of his illustrators, most notably George Cruikshank. And Gardner himself was fond of cartooning: as a child, he illustrated his fledgling stories and "novels"; as a parent, he illustrated the collections of stories he gave to his children. When the firm of Alfred A. Knopf accepted *Grendel* and *The Sunlight Dialogues* for publication, Gardner asked that they and all future works be illustrated, thus creating a textual awareness that would influence the way his books were read.

Gardner's response to Dickens's literary cartoons was anticipated by his response to Walt Disney's animated films, in particular *Snow White and the Seven Dwarfs,* which contained many Gothic elements. In his essay "Cartoons," Gardner writes that between the ages of eight and eighteen he found Dickens and Disney "practically indistinguishable. Both created wonderful cartoon images, told stories as direct as fairy tales, knew the value of broad comedy spiced up with a little weeping."[6] Inspired by these two artists, Gardner "got hooked," he says, by the "grand cartoon" of opera, and by the "cartoon images" of Melville, Milton, and other immortals:

> I'm afraid the embarrassing truth is that the whole literary tradition opened out, for me, from Disney and his kind. I got caught up in the mighty cartoons of Homer and Dante (much later Virgil and Apollonius), the less realistic eighteenth- and nineteenth-century novelists (Fielding, Smollett, Collins, and the rest), the glorious mad Russians (Tolstoy, Dostoevski, Bely), and those kinds of poets who fill one's head with strange, intense visions, like Blake, Coleridge, and Keats. (128)

And during this process Gardner found that—in addition to Dante—"God" had also been "nudging" him toward the *Beowulf* poet, the *Gawain* poet, and Chaucer (129). For Gardner, the great poets of the past created "grotesques (cartoon people and places), noble feeling, humor . . . and real storytelling" (131). They offered him perspectives and literary techniques which he could adapt and make new in objectifying his vision of the contemporary world.

Gardner was not primarily concerned with imitating what he referred to as "so-called reality." Even his seemingly "realistic" novels are touched with Gothic atmosphere and exaggeration. He saw life with a cartoonist's eye and he gave the grotesque a metaphysical as well as an ironic edge. Though some of his best fiction adopted the narrative viewpoint of objective and ironic novelists like Henry Fielding, Gardner's vision was essentially subjective and Gothic. He was intensely conscious of the Romantic tradition of writers like Coleridge, Hawthorne, and Melville, and he mixed the comic with the tragic to create the grotesque tensions familiar to "modernists" like Faulkner, O'Connor, and Saul Bellow, who still affirmed that there were universal truths to be discovered through the process of art.

But Gardner was also inspired by the innovative fiction of contemporaries like John Barth, Donald Barthelme, and William Gass, though they were identified with the term "postmodernism," which Gardner rejected. As he says in *On Moral Fiction,* the term "not only isolates a few writers and praises them beyond their due, depressing the stock of others or willfully misreading them; it judges cynical or nihilistic writers as characteristic of the age, and therefore significant, and thus supports, even celebrates ideas no father would wittingly teach his children."[7]

Unfortunately, Gardner does not distinguish between "cynical" and "nihilistic" writers in *On Moral Fiction,* and this failure to define or restrict his terms, here and elsewhere, blurs his argument. To Gardner, often tempted by suicide,[8] nihilism was a very real threat, and his own innovative fiction attempts to confront the personal despair that nihilism generated. *On Moral Fiction* is not a dispassionate view of contemporary fiction; it is the ambivalent response of a writer who criticizes his contemporaries for addressing their "talents to parody . . ." (54) while he repeatedly indicates elsewhere that a large part of his own fiction depends on parody. Given this and other such contradictions, *On Moral Fiction* does not illuminate John Gardner's fiction so much as it illuminates the psychology of the writer who produced the fiction. Gardner was far more experimental in his approach to fiction than his essentially conservative pronouncements suggest.

Readers should therefore be cautious in approaching the approximately 150 recorded interviews and speeches that Gardner gave during his career.[9] As Robert Boyd noted in an early profile, Gardner "responds freely, talking easily about the motives behind his creations and the effects he is trying to achieve; yet there is a sly offhandedness about his answers and about his readiness to agree with most any observation the interviewer makes."[10] This "offhandedness," sly or ingenuous, may partially account for Gardner's contradictory responses to interviewers. Though the central thesis of *On Moral Fiction* is that fiction should search for "truths to live by," Gardner's earlier statements to interviewers make him sound, by comparison, like one of postmodernists that he was so insistent on rejecting. In an interview occasioned by the publication of *Grendel,* for example, Gardner told Digby Diehl that he had nothing to say except that "words are beautiful," that he was simply a "stylist," and that he was, therefore, like John Barth, Donald Barthelme, Stanley Elkin, Ralph Ellison, and William Gass, "who have nothing to say either." Moreover, he added, the model for them all was Samuel Beckett—which was "ironic," since Beckett descended from James Joyce, "who still thought he could save the world with literature."[11]

But it is even more ironic, given the save-the-world thesis of *On Moral Fiction,* that Gardner should so often sound like his favorite antagonist, Jean-Paul Sartre, in his ultimate rejection of all systems of thought. Gardner's cure for nothingness was not existential engagement, however, as Sartre required, but esthetic engagement—what he refers to in *Jason and Medeia* as "creation *ex nihilo,* bold leap of Art."[12] Like the Romantic poets William Blake and Samuel Taylor Coleridge, like the neo-Romantic poet Wallace Stevens, Gardner placed his faith in the redemptive power of the imagination.[13]

Gardner saw himself as one of the young writers to whom Faulkner addressed his Nobel Prize speech in 1950, encouraging them to write of "the problems of the human heart in conflict with itself which alone can make good writing because only that is worth writing about, worth the agony and the sweat."[14] Gardner's "heart" was indeed in conflict. As suggested, the contradictory voices of *On Moral Fiction,* not to mention those in his fiction, came out of a desperate need to affirm the worth of his own existence—and, of course, his art, as his less sympathetic reviewers were quick to point out. Citing the indebtedness of *On Moral Fiction* to Tolstoy's essay "What is Art?" (26), which equates the moral purpose of art with religion, Gardner observes that "great art celebrates life's potential, offering a vision unmistakably and unsentimentally rooted in love" (83). And since, as his characters repeatedly discover, "all systems fail," only faith in the imagination can defeat the dragon of nihilism by creating "myths a society can live instead of die by . . ." (126).

But though Gardner repeatedly talks of the high moral purpose of art, he also sees it as a game—"a game played against chaos and death, against entropy. It is a tragic game, for those who have the wit to take it seriously, because our side must lose; a comic game—or so a troll might say—because only a clown with sawdust brains would take our side and eagerly join in" (6). To a writer who saw himself as a clown trying to be a human being, and who projected this identity onto his clownlike protagonists, the "game" of art provided a temporary order for his conflicted emotions and ideas. As a postmodernist in technique (though rejecting the term), he repeatedly experimented with metafiction, which he defined as "fiction that, both in style and theme, investigates fiction,"[15] and which inevitably questioned the "modernist" truths or myths he sought to affirm. Gardner argued in *On Moral Fiction* that "true art imitates nature's total process: endless blind experiment . . . and then ruthless selectivity. . . . Art, in sworn opposition to chaos, discovers *by its process* what it can say. That is art's morality" (14). In other words, if the writer earnestly searches for truths about "so-called reality" and the human condition, the process of writing is a moral act—even if, paradoxically, the "truth" the writer discovers is a myth. By contrast, according to Gardner, the game-players generally referred to as postmodernists (John Barth, Thomas Pynchon, et al.) had accepted nihilism, were cynical about the truths of language, and had substituted dark comedy—or the grotesque—for tragedy. As a consequence, Gardner argued, they had detached themselves from the spiritual concerns of humanity and were experimenting with art for art's sake alone.

Overview

Adopting Alfred North Whitehead's vision of the universe as an indivisible, evolving, and organic process, Gardner affirmed—as an act of faith—that all life is ordered by its essential "connectedness." And he repeatedly affirmed humanity's need for connectedness in reaction to the ideas of Sartre, who argued that the self was always self-conscious, and therefore irrevocably "alienated" (or disconnected) from all reality. As Gardner told the novelist Charles Johnson, in explaining the ideas behind *Grendel* and other novels, "connectedness is something you feel or don't feel," and not to feel connectedness is the "ultimate tragedy."[16]

But Gardner's "tragedy" was Sartre's reality. Though Gardner repeatedly said he hated Sartrean existentialism, his hostility was directed primarily toward the ideas and metaphors of Sartre's early work *Being and Nothingness* (1943). Gardner rejected its denial of history and what he felt was its nihilism. He was offended by Sartre's assertion that since God is dead, it follows that humanity is totally free, and all actions therefore permitted. In reaction, Gardner repeatedly parodied Sartre's assertion that humanity should not imitate historical models of virtue but look instead within individual consciousness for a definition of a true self—and act "authentically," rather than in "Bad Faith." He saw Sartre's existentialism as "solipsistic," because it focused on the self in opposition to all other realities—and he repeatedly objectified this "solipsistic existentialism" and its "nihilism" in his fiction, most notably perhaps in *Grendel*.

Gardner aspired to the role of a poet-priest (as characterized by Shelley in *A Defense of Poetry*) who uses his imagination to search for spiritual order and wholeness in emotional (as opposed to rational) truths. He speaks autobiographically of the healing power of fiction toward the end of *On Moral*

Fiction: "Art begins in a wound, an imperfection—a wound inherent in the nature of life itself—and is an attempt either to learn to live with the wound or to heal it. It is the pain of the wound which impels the artist to do his work, and it is the universality of woundedness in the human condition which makes the work of art significant as medicine or distraction" (181). This need was, as Gardner suggests in *On Becoming a Novelist,* a personal one: "A psychological wound is helpful, if it can be kept in partial control, to keep the novelist driven. Some fatal childhood accident for which one feels responsible and can never fully forgive oneself. . . ."[17]

The fatal childhood accident that Gardner had in mind—and for which he could never forgive himself—took place on 4 April 1945, three months short of his twelfth birthday, when he accidentally killed his younger brother Gilbert, who fell under a two-ton cultipacker that Gardner was pulling with a tractor down a road near his parents' farm south of Batavia. Indeed, the "psychological wound" was so traumatic that Gardner relived the horror of the accident in afterflashes and nightmares throughout his life. And he objectified the moment and its residual guilt throughout his fiction, most directly in the story "Redemption," published in *Atlantic Monthly* (May 1977) and collected in *The Art of Living and Other Stories.*[18]

As Gardner says, such a "wound" must "be kept in partial control"; otherwise the writer risks becoming obsessively autobiographical. To turn his own wound into art—to follow its dictates yet sublimate its emotion—Gardner took his controlling metaphor from the pattern of sin and redemption in Coleridge's *The Rime of the Ancient Mariner,* and employed it from his first published novel, *The Resurrection,* to his last, *Mickelsson's Ghosts.* In his poem, Coleridge dramatizes the redemptive power of imaginative sympathy through the An-

cient Mariner's transcendent love for the water snakes. Gardner adopted Coleridge's metaphor of love and grace, and
associated Coleridge's faith in the imagination with that of
Blake, who saw the "imagination" as "God," the "Divine-
Humanity," and the "Divine body of the Lord Jesus,"[19] and
who repeatedly stressed the power of this divine Imagination
to redeem one from the subjective "hell" of existence. When
Gardner was asked, for example, to explain the metaphorical
significance of his frequent allusions to Blake's phrase "dark
Satanic Mills," he immediately associated Blake with Coleridge, and emphasized their mutual faith in the redemptive
power of the imagination to "transform, transvalue reality by
your emotions. It's Coleridge. It's my great daddy Coleridge.
I think that section in *The Resurrection* where [John] Horne
talks about Coleridge is just about as close to the center of
what I come out of as anything. The idea that . . . I shot the
albatross . . . for no reason, instinct, or what, just nothing.
And then blessed them unaware, which is grace, which you
can't control. I think that's Blake too."[20] Though Gardner
pointed to *The Resurrection* to illustrate his use of Coleridge's
poem, he might easily have pointed to other works. Like the
Ancient Mariner, he told his tale more than once, and he repeatedly used variations of Coleridge's metaphor in telling
it.[21]

The conventions of the Gothic tale (or ballad, in *The
Rime of the Ancient Mariner*) allowed Gardner to pursue metaphysical questions without a slavish concern for realistic details of character, event, or setting. As in the Gothic tale,
Gardner's protagonists are psychologically divided and grotesque. Burdened by feelings of guilt, despair, and alienation,
they search for redemption and order—and repeatedly encounter ghosts and/or hallucinations as they move toward a

transcendent—though humanistic—experience of spiritual connectedness.[22]

But Gardner wanted to push his art beyond subjective, if not obsessional, concerns. In the works that followed *Nickel Mountain* and *The Resurrection* he became systematically more ironic and detached,[23] introducing metafictional techniques first in *The Sunlight Dialogues* and even more pervasively in *Grendel* and "The King's Indian." Indeed, in July 1973, shortly after completing "The King's Indian," he echoed his earlier interview with Digby Diehl, telling Joe David Bellamy that he identified with Donald Barthelme, Robert Coover, William Gass, Stanley Elkin, and John Barth; and asserting that "what art ought to do is tell stories which are moment-by-moment wonderful, which are true to human experience, and which in no way explain human experience." The purpose of his fiction, Gardner said, was to create "circus shows. I *don't* think they are trivial. I think anybody who writes the way us guys write is going to be at the mercy of the critics—because we're going to be misunderstood."[24]

Ironically, however, it was Gardner—not the "critics"—who attacked these writers in *On Moral Fiction* (1978), and led to his being misunderstood. In *The Art of Fiction* (1984), by contrast, he offers a positive and radically different assessment of his literary contemporaries. Always a devoted teacher of creative writing, he puts polemics aside and offers a balanced comment on the options for as well as the obligations of an apprentice writer. Though he talks of the need to create a "vivid, uninterrupted dream in the reader's mind" (115), he here reconciles the contradiction between his statements and his practice. In an illuminating chapter on "Metafiction, Deconstruction, and Jazzing Around," he observes that metafiction can be used to investigate and even undermine "fiction's harmful affects'' (87). Metafiction does so, he says here, by creating ''a story that calls attention to its methods and shows the reader what is happening to him as he reads. In this kind of fiction, needless to say, the law of the 'vivid and continuous dream' is no longer operative; on the contrary, the breaks in the dream are as important as the dream'' (87). Despite this support of metafiction, however, Gardner did not interrupt the continuity of the ''dream'' in his fiction after *October Light*. In the later fiction, he returns to the combination of Gothic romance and ''cartoon realism'' that he perfected in *The Sunlight Dialogues* and anticipated in *Nickel Mountain* and *The Resurrection*.

NOTES

1. Richard Locke, ''Grendel Is a Beauty of a Beast,'' *New York Times* 4 Sept. 1971: 19.

2. For an overview and analysis of Gardner's critical reception, see Robert A. Morace, ''John Gardner and His Reviewers,'' *Thor's Hammer: Essays on John Gardner,* ed. Jeff Henderson (Conway: University of Central Arkansas Press, 1985) 17–32.

3. Particularly significant was a review by Sumner Ferris in *Speculum* 52 (Oct. 1977): 970–74, which inspired Peter Prescott's article ''Theft of 'Paraphrase'?'' *Newsweek* 10 Apr. 1978: 94.

4. Ed Christian, ''An Interview with John Gardner,'' *Prairie Schooner* 54 (Winter 1980–1981): 81.

5. John Gardner, *October Light* (New York: Knopf, 1976) 4.

6. John Gardner, ''Cartoons,'' *In Praise of What Persists,* ed. Stephen Berg (New York: Harper & Row, 1983) 127. Parenthetical page references in the text are to this edition.

7. John Gardner, *On Moral Fiction* (New York: Basic Books, 1978) 55–56. Parenthetical page references in the text are to this edition.

8. See, for example, Gardner's comments about suicide to Anna Quindlen, ''Why He Writes,'' *New York Post* 24 Jan. 1977: 25.

9. For a representative selection of twenty important interviews, see Allan Chavkin, ed., *Conversations with John Gardner* (Jackson: University Press of Mississippi, 1990).

10. Robert Boyd, ''A Writer's Offhanded Dazzle,'' *St. Louis Post-Dispatch* 28 Nov. 1973: F2.

11. Digby Diehl, "Medievalist in Illinois Ozarks," *Los Angeles Times* 5 Sept. 1971: 43.

12. John Gardner, *Jason and Medeia* (New York: Knopf, 1973) 353.

13. For a detailed analysis of the philosophical and esthetic influences on Gardner's "moral" vision, see Per Winther, *The Art of John Gardner: Instruction and Exploration* (Albany: State University of New York Press, 1992) 31–65.

14. James B. Meriwether, ed., *Essays, Speeches & Public Letters,* (New York: Random House, 1965) 119.

15. John Gardner, *The Art of Fiction: Notes on Craft for Young Writers* (New York: Knopf, 1984) 86. Parenthetical page references in the text are to this edition.

16. Chuck [Charles] Johnson, "John Gardner: Author: 'That Rare Creature, a Philosophical Novelist,' " *Southern Illinoisan* [Carbondale] 21 Jan. 1973: A3.

17. John Gardner, *On Becoming a Novelist* (New York: Harper & Row, 1983) 62.

18. See John M. Howell, "The Wound and the Albatross: John Gardner's Apprenticeship," *Thor's Hammer: Essays on John Gardner,* ed. Jeff Henderson (Conway: University of Central Arkansas Press, 1985) 1–16.

19. S. Foster Damon, *A Blake Dictionary: The Ideas and Symbols of William Blake* (1965; Boulder, Colo.: Shambhala Publications, 1979) 195.

20. John Gardner, interview with author, Susquehanna, Pa., 6 August 1980. By permission of the Estate of John Gardner and Georges Borchardt, Inc.

21. See Jeff Henderson, "The Avenues of Mundane Salvation: Time and Change in the Fiction of John Gardner," *American Literature* 55 (Dec. 1983): 611–33.

22. Henderson refers to Gardner's moments of humanistic transcendence and/or redemption as "mundane salvation" (see note 21 above). Gregory L. Morris refers to these moments as products of Gardner's "emotional metaphysics"; see Morris, *A World of Order and Light: The Fiction of John Gardner* (Athens: University of Georgia Press, 1984) 1–4.

23. See Susan Strehle, "John Gardner's Novels: Affirmation and the Alien," *Critique* 18:2 (1976): 86–96.

24. Joe David Bellamy and Pat Ensworth, "John Gardner," *The New Fiction: Interviews with Innovative American Writers,* ed. Joe David Bellamy (Urbana: University of Illinois Press, 1974) 180, 182.

CHAPTER TWO

"Apprentice" Novels

John Gardner's fiction was not published in the order written. To understand the development of his literary themes and forms, his fiction is best considered in the order it was composed. *Nickel Mountain* is a case in point. Gardner had published an early version of the seminal story, "Nickel Mountain," in a student magazine in 1955, and in 1965 he had submitted a revision of the story, along with eight other stories, to New American Library, which had agreed to publish *The Resurrection* (1966). But when New American Library rejected the collection, he put it aside until the early 1970s.

Nickel Mountain: A Pastoral Novel

Gardner always thought of *Nickel Mountain,* like *The Resurrection,* as an "apprentice" novel.[1] After completing *Grendel* (1971), *The Sunlight Dialogues* (1972), and other works, Gardner revised the "Nickel Mountain" collection and called it *Nickel Mountain: A Pastoral Novel*. To make the collection read more like a "novel," he cut one unrelated story ("The Joy of the Just"), and tightened the narrative progression of the eight remaining stories, or chapters: "Nickel Mountain," "The Wedding," "The Edge of the Woods," "The Things," "The Devil," "Nimrod's Tower," "The Meeting," and, finally, "The Grave," which he extensively revised to give the novel a lingering and attenuated vision of the protagonist, Henry Soames, who knows he will soon die.

Illustrated with etchings by Thomas O'Donohue, *Nickel Mountain* tells how Henry, a monstrously fat man in his early forties with a bad heart, is resurrected spiritually after he marries seventeen-year-old Callie Wells, who is pregnant by Willard Freund, the young son of a wealthy farmer. But despite its sentimental premise, *Nickel Mountain* offers poetic and moving portraits of its characters and their problems. Gardner's most realistic and accessible work of fiction, *Nickel Mountain* has endured in popularity, starting with many weeks on the best-sellers lists in America, and continuing in paperback printings and foreign translations.

Nickel Mountain's rural (or "pastoral") characters resemble those in Sherwood Anderson's episodic novel *Winesburg, Ohio* (1919), which was similarly built from stories. Henry Soames echoes, for example, the compulsive talking and gestures of Wing Biddlebaum, the protagonist of Anderson's story "Hands." And Gardner reveals his conscious indebtedness to Anderson, as well as his instinct for parody, with the given names of Henry's closest friends and antagonists, George Loomis and Willard Freund—an ironic salute to Anderson's recurring protagonist, George Willard.

The novel begins in December 1954, and reflects the social values of the 1950s. In the first chapter, "Nickel Mountain," which is self-contained and reflects its origins as a story, Gardner establishes the novel's basic conflict and situation: Henry Soames, bearlike, lumbering, overweight, has had a heart attack; and unless he loses ninety pounds, he has less than a year to live. Frightened of life as well as death, he eats compulsively and talks compulsively to lonely truckers and despairing friends like George Loomis. They come at all hours to the Stop-Off Cafe, which Henry owns and operates on a highway in the Catskills north of Nickel Mountain and south of the town of Slater—Gardner's fictional transformation of Batavia, New York.

When Henry hires sixteen-year-old Calliope ("Callie") Wells to work as a waitress, his life miraculously changes. She appears, "as if by magic, like a crocus where yesterday there'd been snow,"[2] though she is not conventionally pretty, but instead tall, like her father, and with the "same hand-whittled look, the squareness of nose, cheeks, and ears" (8). But Henry grows to care for her. When she becomes pregnant, and Willard Freund will not accept responsibility, Henry offers George Loomis money to marry her. When George refuses, Henry has a mild heart attack, and during his recovery Callie grows to care for him, though she probably does not love him.

When Callie reveals her feelings to Henry, his response is characteristically grotesque: with "lips trembling, stretching out like a sad clown's" (57), he tells her he loves her and wants to marry her. Soon after, Callie beside him, Henry heads his old Ford south on Highway 98, to ask permission of her father, a man younger than himself. He has transcended his spiritual isolation in a resurrection of emotion which Gardner objectifies in one of the novel's most poignant metaphors: "Her head on his shoulder was pleasantly heavy; heavy enough, almost, to crush bone" (59).

"The Wedding" focuses on Callie's viewpoint and her conflicting emotions as she prepares for her marriage to Henry—the very antithesis of a young girl's dream. Dressed in an old Welsh wedding gown, Callie is surrounded by gifts and flooded by memories and misgivings. As in his story "Come on Back" (*The Art of Living and Other Stories*), Gardner draws on the Welsh family background of his mother (nee

Priscilla Jones), and projects himself as Callie: "All the relatives were assembled, mostly from her mother's side, more Joneses and Thomases and Griffiths than she'd seen in one place in all her life. It was like an Eisteddfodd or a Gymanfa Ganu" (67).

Callie panics at the thought that she is about to marry an unattractive man more than twice her age, and she wants to run. But when her uncle John tells her in Welsh, "Grace be with you" (81), she experiences a spiritual transcendence. As she moves down the aisle toward the altar, she becomes one of Gardner's moral artists, feeling an intense love and transmuting all she sees into beauty—even Henry, who appears "comically beautiful, as all her own family were beautiful, and she walked slowly, . . . knowing that she too was beautiful . . ." (83).

In a stylistic contrast to the intense lyricism of Callie's story, Gardner narrates "The Edge of the Woods" from Henry's perspective, using bluntly naturalistic details. Henry has long feared that Willard Freund will walk out of the ominously dark woods and claim Callie and her baby. But Henry shares Callie's pregnancy, enduring her suffering as well as her rage. And with tears flowing, he shares her joy as a parent. He realizes ultimately that the baby (Jimmy) with the "forceps scars" is his spiritual son: "You had to be there, and Willard Freund hadn't been, and now there was no place left for him, no love, no hate . . ." (123).

Henry loses his fear of the woods. They are now, he decides, Willard's prison, a symbol of his alienation. By contrast, Henry—a father as well as a husband—gains the courage to be, and temporarily overcomes his compulsive eating and frightening obsessions. He finds redemption, like so many of Gardner's characters to come, in a transcendence of self through the joy of spiritual connectedness with other human beings.

Building a thematic contrast to Henry's discovery of connectedness, Gardner focuses "The Things" (reprinted in *Prize Stories 1974*) on George Loomis's discovery of the spiritual void within himself. George has not only had a leg shattered in Korea, he has recently lost an arm in a farm accident, and his physical wounds (like Henry's damaged heart) suggest his psychological wounds. Bitter, cynical, moving inevitably toward nihilism, George lives well away from town on Crow Mountain in a brooding fourteen-room house that belonged to his deceased parents. Instead of making friends, George collects "things"—scarce, antique objects of all kinds, which other collectors value but which he will not sell. Things are George's substitute for people. Though he was brave under fire in Korea, he will always be afraid of emotional involvement; instead of love, he has "things."

Gardner dramatizes George's self-discovery in a memorable scene of counterpointed imagery and escalating suspense. When George drives his truck away from Henry's house, he retains an idyllic image of Callie, with Jimmy on her arm, waving in an aura of light, and Henry standing beside her "like a balding upright bear with one paw on her shoulder, waving too" (127). By contrast, George's house looms up ominously, and he is already apprehensive. There has been a murder in the area, a car has just swerved at him out of nowhere, and a recent encounter with a (supposedly) blind collector has made him afraid for his "things." When he slams the truck door, the stillness echoes and surrounds him, and he immediately feels that someone is watching. Grabbing a rifle from the shed, he crawls through the mud and bursts into the house—only to discover that it is as empty as his life. Humiliated, he realizes that if Henry had done the same foolish thing, "even if it had been all delusion, the mock heroics of a helmeted clown, it would have counted" (141). But his own "clown"-like action (a pervasive metaphor of humanity in Gardner's fiction) does not count: there is no one to whom it matters.

As in the previous stories, the governing theme is the transcendence of the self through the connectedness of love and community. Like Henry, George Loomis is a grotesque whose emotional state is objectified by his disfigured body. But Henry ultimately gains his humanity because he cares about people and believes in the holiness of life. George, by contrast, has no faith in life, and drifts still further toward nihilism.

In an ironic counterpoint to George's nihilism, "The Devil" focuses on the distorted faith of Simon Bale, a Jehovah's Witness whose exploitation of Henry Soames's goodwill is so extreme that it produces the kind of grotesque outrage that moves the dark comedy of Faulkner's *As I Lay Dying*, one of Gardner's favorite novels. Bale's fanatical proselytizing so alienates the community that it is ready to believe he set the fire that burned down his house and destroyed his wife. But Henry has faith in Simon and, much against Callie's wishes, not only takes Simon into his house but pays for his wife's funeral. Even when Simon's incessant sermonizing drives customers away from the Stop-Off, Henry simply watches in quiet anguish. But when Simon so frightens little Jimmy with tales of hellfire that he screams he has seen the "devil," Henry screams in turn at Simon, who falls backward down a flight of stairs to his death. A year or so earlier Henry had awakened just in time to catch Jimmy from falling while he was sleepwalking. Jimmy had immediately forgotten the incident but "for Henry the memory of that night was like a wound that would never heal" (201).

Henry's wound is deepened when he fails to prevent Simon's fall, and Gardner, building on the emotional trauma and guilt he experienced over the death of his younger brother, Gilbert,[3] explores Henry's wound at length, echoing and counterpointing his trauma through the characters of George Loomis and Willard Freund. Though "Nimrod's Tower" is ostensibly concerned with themes of love, responsibility, and humility, Henry's wound is still the dominant concern. In speaking to George Loomis of Simon's death, for example, Henry tells him, "I keep seeing it over and over, George. I see it clearer even than it was, slowed down, like a movie. I see that look on his face, and me moving toward him, shouting at him, and it seems to me I have a choice, whether to keep on shouting or not, and I choose, I keep shouting, and then all at once he falls" (237).

Henry's failure *to choose* to stop "shouting" becomes for him a sin of omission, and—here as in most of his fiction—Gardner develops the theme of guilt in relation to ideas of free will and determinism. Henry says he had a choice, but it is clear that rage determined his action—that he was ruled by compulsion. Yet not to make a choice is to function at the level of a beast, and—as the monster Grendel is so agonizingly aware—there is no redemption for a beast without free will or conscience. But Henry cannot escape the trauma either; he keeps reliving the moment in different situations and insisting he had a "choice." He cannot accept the dismal alternative: if he had no choice, and Simon's death was only an accident—or simply "chance," as George insists—then the world has no meaning and the God he has affirmed all his life is dead. Indeed, George insists that Henry is not suffering from guilt at all but from the "horror" that Simon's death was meaningless, thereby making Henry's life meaningless. But as Gardner later reveals, George is more in despair than Henry, since he has accidentally killed the eccentric creature known as the "Goat Lady." Essentially, he is pleading for his own lack of moral responsibility as much as he is for Henry's. But in doing so, George only succeeds in denying his humanity. He does not ease the trauma of when, in counterpoint to Henry, he feels "the memory of the accident coming over him . . ." (256).

To find redemption, George must sacrifice his pride and, in total selflessness, confess his guilt to Henry and Callie. Instead, he denies knowledge of the Goat Lady in such a guilty manner that Henry emulates Coleridge's Ancient Mariner by blessing him "unaware": "Henry looked at him, pitying him, George Loomis no more free than a river or a wind, and, as if unaware that he was doing it, Henry broke the cookie in his hand and let the pieces fall. She [Callie] realized with a start that it was final: George had saved them after all" (261). Henry symbolically "breaks bread" and receives grace. In Coleridgean terms, he is redeemed by his imagination. He imagines what George feels and, through his complete empathy and sympathy, he transcends his own isolating guilt. George, on the other hand, retreats into his pride and even greater isolation and despair, unable to forgive himself, unable to accept the forgiveness of others, and thus totally the victim of an emotional determinism: ". . . no more free than a river or a wind." By contrast, Henry has renounced all pride.

As before, Gardner diffuses Henry's reactions in objectifying the moment of redemption, in this instance focusing on Callie and moving toward the supernatural. Convinced that George has "saved them," Callie finds herself weightless and faint—and hears a voice whisper that "all shall be saved. . . . *Even the sticks and stones*" (261). Overwhelmed by this feeling of universal sentience, she anticipates similar moments of grace in later novels—especially *Mickelsson's Ghosts*—when she sees the ghosts of Simon Bale, Henry's father, her great-great-grandfather, and her uncle John, as well as "a hundred more she didn't know, solemn and full of triumphant joy" (261), stretching from the diner to the woods and beyond. Then the vision is gone and she is left with Henry "in the amazing stillness" (262)—a metaphorical echo of the hymn "Amazing Grace."

In building a novel out of short stories, Gardner encountered problems of thematic resolution as well as repetition. Since Henry is the protagonist, the novel might well have ended with his moment of spiritual connection, which Gardner equated with secular redemption and "grace." But the character of Willard Freund—crucial to the lives of Henry and Callie—has not been accounted for.

To round out the novel and tie up the plot strands, Gardner adds "The Meeting." Set three years after Jimmy's birth, the story describes Willard's return home from college at Christmas. Having hitched a ride during a heavy snowfall, he is sitting half-asleep in the car when he imagines the driver is going to hit a snowplow. After he yells "Look out!" (279), the terrified driver swerves the car sideways into snowplow's path and fantasy becomes reality, leaving Willard, like Henry Soames and George Loomis, involuntarily responsible for a fatal accident. And like them, he experiences a symbolic projection of Gardner's own childhood "wound," seeing the "accident again and again, as though his mind could not get free of it" (282).

But despite his traumatic reaction, Willard takes no responsibility, just as he took no responsibility for Callie's baby. Though he feels embarrassed and guilty when he meets Henry and Callie (with Jimmy) at Llewellyn's store in Slater, their goodwill fills him with "crazy joy" (289). And in an epiphany characteristic of *Winesburg, Ohio* he tells himself: "I was insane. . . . It's as simple as that! I must remember, from now on. Whatever happens, I must remember" (289).

Having accounted for Willard Freund, Gardner ends with "The Grave," which functions as a coda—a moving attenuation of Henry's life and his tranquil perceptions of its meaning. He and Jimmy, now four, watch the exhumation of a boy who had died at fourteen, some fifty years earlier. As he listens to the boy's grieving parents, Henry is conscious of his own spiritual exhumation from the lean-to room behind the Stop-Off, which Callie has now renamed "The Maples" and expanded into a handsome restaurant.

Henry has given himself up to Callie, whose benevolent domination parallels (and illuminates) Beowulf's paradoxically benevolent domination of Gardner's Grendel. Like Grendel in the moments before his death, Henry chooses to accept what he cannot prevent from happening, and experiences the "sudden joy" of connectedness. He muses "like a man only half-awake on how it had all come about, the long train of trivial accidents, affirmed one by one, that made a man's life what it happened to become" (300). He has, in the spirit of the medieval philosopher Boethius, denied false pride, reconciled the forces of determinism and free will, and become, in the end, "mystical," thus beyond the need for words, because the "very separateness of words was contrary to what he seemed to know" (301). Like Callie on her wedding day, he feels "born again" and he transcends the separation of self and world, "his vision not something apart from the world but the world itself transmuted" (301). George Loomis has collected lifeless "things" in his lifeless house; Henry has discovered the "holiness of things . . . the idea of magical change" (302). And like Callie, he hears a voice whispering of a universal sentience, and he has "a vision of dust succinct with spirit, God inside wasps, oak trees, people, chickens walking in the yard" (303). Though he knows he will soon die, and that Callie and Jimmy will grieve his death, he is tired now, and he thinks ambiguously of "how good it would be to lie down, only for a little while, and rest."

In writing the stories of *Nickel Mountain,* Gardner was serving an apprenticeship, exploring narrative structures and techniques and learning as he proceeded. He was concerned, like Anderson, with objectifying the psychological truths of characters who become grotesque when they fix on single truths at the expense of all others. But unlike Anderson, Gardner treats his unsophisticated characters without irony, even though they think and speak in cliches. He develops his variations on the theme of guilt and redemption in the same spirit, using a simple and direct style, elaborating and counterpointing the theme from chapter to chapter, and generally narrating from the third-person limited viewpoint—a strategy he later regretted.

By focusing on the subjective feelings and thoughts of a single character, Gardner tried to develop that character in a short space while controlling the shape and development of the narrative. Thus in the first four chapters of *Nickel Mountain* he used the third-person limited (or subjective) viewpoint of each story's protagonist. In the next two stories ("The Devil" and "Nimrod's Tower"), however, he switched to an omniscient viewpoint. This viewpoint allowed him to stand back from the characters and write about them at an emotional distance, then move in to give a subjective perspective, and then back out again (like a motion picture camera) to give an overview of the total action. After creating this psychological distance, he returned in the final stories ("The Meeting" and "The Grave") to the third-person limited viewpoint. Yet he was still unhappy with the tone: since the characters are essentially provincial, seldom introspective, and, with the exception of George Loomis, rarely detached or ironic about themselves, he felt that the emotionally restricted portraits created sentimentality,[4] and he tried to avoid the problem of narrative subjectivity in *The Resurrection*.

The Resurrection

A sharp contrast to *Nickel Mountain,* with its relatively simple characters, subjective viewpoint, and episodic structure, *The Resurrection* is a novel of ideas with intellectually complicated characters whose thoughts and actions are described from the viewpoint of an omniscient narrator in a strongly causal and symmetrical plot. Published by New American Library in 1966 (and reprinted by Ballantine Books, with minor stylistic changes, in 1974), it was Gardner's first attempt at a "philosophical" novel.

Like Henry Soames, James Chandler is resurrected from his spiritual isolation shortly before dying. As in *Nickel Mountain,* Gardner creates a Gothic atmosphere, using Chandler's psychological trauma to motivate and justify the presence of ghosts and/or hallucinations. But the tone is radically different from that of the earlier novel, and Chandler's moment of redemption is tragicomic if not grotesque.

James Chandler is tenured as an associate professor of philosophy at Stanford University. Having suffered more than he can admit from his father's cold-blooded rationalism and ultimate suicide, Chandler has retreated from life into the world of ideas. Described as "a pallid, owl-faced, professorial little man in thick glasses,"[5] he has been so successful in his retreat that he barely knows his three young daughters and does not really understand his wife. Chandler, in the same spirit as the postmodernist fiction writers that Gardner later mocked in *On Moral Fiction,* has just spent two years on a long monograph entitled "Am I Now Dreaming?" It was, he tells himself, "at bottom no more—or less—than an immensely elaborate joke on the idea of philosophy itself, a complement to his more serious *Philosophy as Pure Technique*" (7). But suddenly he is shocked awake by the joke life has played on him: he has aleukemic leukemia, it is on the verge of the "blast crisis," and unless it goes into remission, which is doubtful, he will be dead in three weeks.

According to Gardner, the initial impetus for writing *The Resurrection* was his negative reaction to Tolstoy's last novel *Resurrection* (1899). Gardner could not accept Tolstoy's rejection of "rote behavior" in religion, and he set out to show why Tolstoy was wrong. In doing so, he developed a parallel between Chandler's philosophical idealism and estheticism and that of the English philosopher and historian R. G. Collingwood.[6] Like Collingwood—or at least Collingwood early in his career—Chandler is a metaphysician, a self-consciously old-fashioned philosopher concerned with questioning the nature of reality and the structure of the universe. And just as Collingwood, debilitated by cerebral strokes, tried to finish a certain body of work while he could still concentrate, so also does Chandler, though in a matter of weeks rather than years. In his final days Chandler struggles to focus his thoughts and write an essay which refutes Kant's thesis that beauty is divorced from ethical, moral, or practical rewards. Anticipating *On Moral Fiction,* Chandler argues that beauty in art cannot be divorced from its moral impact on the beholder.

When he learns of his terminal illness Chandler returns to his hometown of Batavia, New York. It is April and the trees are in bud. Sleeping in his mother's house after a long absence, he is filled with memories of his youth—of his grandfather's farm, of troubled moments with his father, of happy moments with his uncle John E. Jones (Callie's uncle in *Nickel Mountain*). Though he has little energy, he walks the streets of the town, exploring old haunts, meeting old friends.

The working title for *The Resurrection* was "When the Jingling Stops." This phrase alludes to the novel's central metaphor, which Gardner establishes with the poignant image of blind children playing baseball. Their baseball has a bell on it so they can follow its flight. As Chandler and his daughters watch, the ball is hit, and it flies, "a bright patch of white, a nagging innocent jingle" (47), over the pitcher's head. While the fielders stand motionless, heads cocked, listening for the bell, the batter runs, following a guide string around the bases. When the ball comes to rest, the jingling stops, and Chandler is profoundly moved by the reaction of the frustrated players to the "absolute stillness. Slowly, like children in a trance or like people moving underwater, the players on both teams began to move in the direction of center field. Just beyond second base they got down on hands and knees and began to grope in the grass, soundlessly, mechanically, as if without hope" (47). Chandler ultimately relates this vision to his concept of moral art, anticipating Gardner's primary assertion in *On Moral Fiction* that art is "a game played against chaos and death, against entropy."[7] Though Chandler never articulates the game metaphor directly, it hovers in his imagination, and Gardner uses it to control and inform the clownlike actions of James Chandler, Emma Staley (a senile artist), Viola Staley (Emma's nineteen-year-old niece), and John Horne (a law librarian and amateur philosopher). Each character acts the role of a grotesque clown and momentarily turns life into art.

Chandler fears the "lawless proliferation of lymphatic-type cells" (13) within him, and he thinks of their ultimate explosion as his "cosmic detonation." At the same time, he is haunted—both awake and asleep—by the "ghost" of an "old woman," a projection of his existential terror. And when Viola Staley's aunt Emma touches his "cheek very lightly with her dry, cold fingers" (62), he immediately recalls the old woman of his fantasies and dreams. Aunt Emma is, in fact, Chandler's grotesque muse. Though her painting *The Old Mill* is "torturously rendered," it gives him the "sense of sudden release, unexpected joy, that one experienced in the presence of true works of art" (166). It temporarily orders his chaotic emotions and allows him to defend himself against the nightmare of exploding cells. Aunt Emma has "painted the soul's sublime acceptance of lawless, proliferating substance: things and their motions" (166–67). Moved by the painting and its mindless creator, Chandler thinks of Wallace Stevens's poem "Connoisseur of Chaos":

> *A. A violent order is disorder; and*
> *B. A great disorder is an order. These*
> *Two things are one. . . .* (167)

Associating the game, the painting, and the poem, Chandler echoes Gardner's esthetic theory that moral art grows out of the defiance of chaos and the search for order: "All that belongs in Burke's realm of *the Sublime* (the large, the angular, the terrifying, etc.) we may identify with *moral affirmation;* that is to say, with human *defiance of chaos* . . ." (201). And this equation of the "defiance of chaos" with "moral affirmation" leads Chandler to conclude that the "highest state a man can achieve is one of *aesthetic wholeness . . .*" (202), the state which Chandler apparently achieves at the point of death.

Crucial to the novel's explication of this and other esthetic theories is the character of John Horne. Like Chandler, Horne is a patient in the hospital and, as he says, "dying, or so my doctor has decreed" (236). Like Henry Soames, Horne is obese and clownlike, but far more grotesque. Using Horne's character as a seemingly untrustworthy teller of truths, Gardner has him introduce, sometimes by negative assertion, the novel's major themes and motifs. Horne tells Chandler's wife, Marie, that "life can be resurrected . . ." (120), and he tells Chandler—who was hoping for a dialogue on the morality of art—that man "must be born again . . ." (147), but that he can only be reborn through the accident of "grace" which Coleridge's hero experiences in *The Rime of the Ancient Mariner.* According to Horne—and Gardner, who later endorsed Horne's interpretation in an interview[8]—the Mariner shoots the albatross, "symbolically crucifying Christ out of sheer indifference" (148), and then, "with no more conscious volition than ever—*not* because of his atonement, no, out of utter absurdity—he saves himself by blessing [the water snakes] 'unaware' " (149).

Gardner develops the idea of redemption—here and in later works—by equating Coleridge's metaphorical "water snakes" with Friedrich Nietzsche's metaphorical "herd"—his contemptuous term for the common man. Horne introduces Nietzsche's metaphor when he says that he has "no interest whatever in the pastures of the herd, some cheap and miserable consolation" (150), and when he tells Chandler that he is "unlike the common herd" (180). But when Chandler rejects him, Horne, in an ironic reversal, immediately identifies with the "herd" he has just rejected, telling himself that

Chandler is acting out of "pride," out of a greater concern with his own "private welfare than with the welfare of the whole" (182).

Since Chandler refuses to talk to Horne after their failed dialogue, Horne forces Miss Thomas, an elderly blind acquaintance, to act as Chandler's surrogate. In talking to Chandler, he affirmed ideals that he desperately wants to believe. In talking to Miss Thomas, however, he takes on the persona of a Sartrean existentialist, echoing *Being and Nothingness* and anticipating the nihilistic protagonists of *The Sunlight Dialogues, The Wreckage of Agathon,* and *Grendel,* as well as the dialogue structure that Gardner would employ in these later novels.

Like the Sunlight Man and Agathon, Horne asks how he could make a "leap of faith," since "time and space are a bucket of worms?" (236). And like Grendel, he asks,

> "What do I do? I play the creature in his death throes. Because I can't realize it, of course. . . . I look at the world and I brood on it, but nothing I see or brood on is there, only some unimaginable distortion, the reality behind the mask. I say that the sky is black tonight, but it has no interest in being the black I see. . . . So much for human consciousness. An ingenious and delicate instrument designed by monstrous reaches of time for the sole purpose of knowing that all it knows is wrong and, anyway, irrelevant." (236–37)

Though Horne further outrages Miss Thomas with sacrilegious comments that reflect his self-pity and existential terror, the ultimate importance of his monologue is its progress toward nihilism and its counterpointing of Chandler's absurd heroism.

Like Horne, Chandler has isolated himself from emotional involvement by retreating into the world of abstraction.

His isolation is violated, however, by Viola Staley, whose "emerald" green eyes are so hypnotic that Chandler cannot tell "whether a thing so unnatural was beautiful or terrible" (51). When Viola discovers that she "loves" the cadaverous and dying Chandler, she sees herself "with perfect clarity as grotesque, comic, a ragged lady clown in a broken bicycle routine" (213). But, overwhelmed by the romance of his imminent death, she kisses him, says she loves him, and tells herself melodramatically that she has come to "*kill him!*" (225). Then, comparing herself to "someone in a movie," she tells him she has left Aunt Emma alone. When Chandler does not reprimand her, she is overwhelmed with gratitude—and, in a reversal of the Ancient Mariner's blessing of the water snakes (a reversal echoed in "The King's Indian"), she decides that the cadaverous man is "*beautiful*," loves him "more than ever," and says to him, "God bless you, Mr. Chandler" (225).

In reaction, Chandler—stunned as well as blessed, his emotional isolation penetrated—feels intensely alive, spiritually resurrected. Previously he has, as John Horne suggests, rejected the Nietzschean "herd" for the beauty of abstraction. But only by blessing the "herd"—Gardner's analogue for Coleridge's water snakes—can Chandler, like the Mariner, experience the accident of grace: "All this time it had been there right in front of him—if it had been a snake it would have bit him—and he'd missed it! It was not the beauty of the world one must affirm but *the world,* the buzzing, blooming confusion itself. He had slipped from celebrating what was to the celebration of empty celebration. *To keep a drowsy emperor awake*" (229). The green-eyed Viola is, metaphorically, the "snake" that bit him. She blesses Chandler, and he blesses her in return as the very personification of the "buzzing, blooming confusion'' that is life. Previously, like W. B. Yeats's persona in ''Sailing to Byzantium,'' he had celebrated the kind of beautiful abstractions that might, as Yeats says, ''keep a drowsy emperor awake.'' But now Chandler recognizes that *''one must make life art''* (229).

This is precisely what Chandler does in Gardner's elaborately symbolic and thematically ambiguous ending. Moved by Viola's violent declaration of love, Chandler literally sacrifices his life for art by making a gesture even more melodramatic and absurd than her own. Following Viola to the Staley house, he tells himself madly that he is making a pilgrimage *''for Art's sake. As the play requires. We shall set our face to Jerusalem''* (229).

Meanwhile, in counterpoint to Chandler's action, senile Aunt Emma, her mind an even greater chaos, resurrects her spirit from its death-in-life by escaping the unguarded house and heading toward the world of *The Old Mill*—the painting which Chandler associates with the blind children and the jingling baseball. Echoing the symbolism of the game, Gardner has Emma pick up a ''small silver bell'' and, smiling ''like a fox,'' sneak out of the house, where she ''frees the bell and lets it jingle softly'' (227) as she heads along the Tonawanda Creek toward the flatland where the cattails grow, and where, Gardner suggests, the jingling stops in some undefined fatality.

Like Aunt Emma, Chandler fulfills Horne's notion of a redemption that comes from an act of ''utter absurdity'' (149), as he watches himself struggle ''like some grotesque vaudeville clown'' (230) up the steps of the Staley house and crawl to Viola's feet. As his death by ''cosmic detonation'' begins, the room grows ''brighter, almost blinding, as though the old woman were emerging from every atom of the place at once''

(232). And in counterpoint to Viola's melodramatic image of herself as a heroine in a movie, Chandler imagines he is a cowboy "out of some grim, high-class Western . . ." (232).

Chandler wants to tell Viola that their movie melodrama has done "no harm. It's done us no harm" (232). But in fact, most readers assume that the embarrassing circumstances of Chandler's death would (in fiction as in life) do a great deal of harm to his wife and daughters. Indeed, Gardner condemned Chandler's action himself in 1978,[9] and critics have understandably interpreted the ending in light of Gardner's extraliterary comments.[10] At the time he wrote the novel, however, Gardner was apparently more concerned about dramatizing Chandler's rebirth into the joy of "aesthetic wholeness,"[11] than he was about the reaction of Chandler's wife to the potentially embarrassing circumstances of his death, since any such reactions lay beyond the novel's temporal boundaries. Instead, his emphasis in the novel is on what Gardner, in 1980, called Chandler's "intense love without attachment"[12] toward all humanity.

Ultimately, a narrative passage in *Mickelsson's Ghosts* offers a more reliable gloss on the symbolism of Chandler's climactic action than do Gardner's extraliterary comments. Like Chandler, Peter Mickelsson is a mad philosophy instructor who suffers from hallucinations (or "ghosts"); like Chandler, he experiences "grace" when inspired by sexual love. Shortly before Mickelsson's redemptive moment, Gardner's narrative reports that "Nietzsche had, in his final great madness, debased himself, throwing himself down, to no avail, before Cosima Wagner, admitting at last, symbolically, however futilely, the necessity of what he'd dismissed from his system, amazing grace. . . ."[13] In his madness Chandler, like Mickelsson, imitates Nietzsche's grotesque action and experiences the "amazing grace" that Nietzsche had dismissed, and that

Gardner, in both *The Resurrection* and *Mickelsson's Ghosts,* synthesizes with the redemption of the Ancient Mariner. In crawling like a cowboy "out of some grim, high-class Western" and reaching out in death to touch Viola's foot, Chandler is not only, like Nietzsche, debasing himself before the woman he thinks (in his madness) he loves, he is symbolically blessing the Nietzschean "herd," which Gardner equates with Coleridge's water snakes.

Gardner introduces *The Resurrection* with a brief prologue describing visits over the years to Chandler's grave by the women in his life: his mother; his wife, Marie; his daughter Karen; and Viola. This prologue establishes the novel's elegiac tone and defines the voice of its omniscient narrator. To complete the frame, Gardner returns (in the final chapter) to the perspective of Marie and Karen, who attend Emma's sister Betsy Staley's concert at the Y.M.C.A. auditorium. At the moment of Chandler's death, Marie and Karen are listening to Aunt Betsy (who is very deaf) attack the piano keys in a musical counterpoint to Chandler's "cosmic detonation," which Gardner here translates into a "terrible holocaust of chords and runs, each note precise, overpowering, irremissible—not music but a monstrous retribution of sound, the mindless roar of things in motion, on the meddlesome mind of man" (243). And with the irony of this alliterative prose poetry, Gardner completes the novel's three-part narrative, which focuses on Chandler's thoughts in all twelve chapters of part 1, but only in six chapters of part 2, and only in three chapters of part 3, where he exists almost entirely in the consciousness and memories of others, and thus achieves a kind of spiritual resurrection, if not immortality.

The Resurrection was Gardner's first attempt at what he called a "philosophical novel," and it offers an excellent introduction to his major fiction. Though the novel sometimes states rather than dramatizes the philosophical ideas that moved him, and though its structure is sometimes arbitrary rather than organic, the characters and the situations are well realized, and the narrative style is poetic and evocative. *The Resurrection* marked a strong beginning and its themes, metaphors, and symbols directly anticipate and illuminate *The Sunlight Dialogues* and *Grendel*.

NOTES

1. John Gardner, interview with author, Susquehanna, Pa., 6 August 1980. By permission of the Estate of John Gardner and Georges Borchardt, Inc.

2. John Gardner, *Nickel Mountain: A Pastoral Novel* (New York: Knopf, 1973) 7. Parenthetical page references in the text are to this edition.

3. For a more detailed discussion of Gardner's "wound" in this novel, *The Resurrection,* the posthumously published novel "Stillness," and the story "Redemption," see John M. Howell, "The Wound and the Albatross: John Gardner's Apprenticeship," *Thor's Hammer: Essays on John Gardner,* ed. Jeff Henderson (Conway: University of Central Arkansas Press, 1985) 1–15.

4. John Gardner, interview with author.

5. John Gardner, *The Resurrection* (1966; rev. ed., New York: Ballantine Books, 1974) 8. Parenthetical page references in the text are to this paperback edition, which contains incidental stylistic changes and reflects Gardner's final intention.

6. See Gregory L. Morris's discussion of Tolstoy and Collingwood in Morris, *A World of Order and Light: The Fiction of John Gardner* (Athens: University of Georgia Press, 1984) 22–24.

7. John Gardner, *On Moral Fiction* (New York: Basic Books, 1978) 6. Parenthetical page references in the text are to this edition.

8. John Gardner, interview with author.

9. See Ed Christian, "An Interview with John Gardner," *Prairie Schooner* 54 (Winter 1980–1981): 74, where Gardner says, "Everything's gone horrible; the old lady has wandered off into the night, and so his attempt to turn death into life misfires horribly."

10. See, for example, Morris 36–37.

11. For a discussion of this and other contradictory aspects of this novel, see Leonard Butts, *The Novels of John Gardner: Making Life Art as a Moral Process* (Baton Rouge: Louisiana State University Press, 1988) 1–15.

Notes

12. John Gardner, interview with author.
13. John Gardner, *Mickelsson's Ghosts* (New York: Knopf, 1982) 578.

CHAPTER THREE

The Sunlight Dialogues

*T*he *Sunlight Dialogues* (1972), like *The Resurrection,* is set in Batavia and develops similar themes. Gardner began *The Sunlight Dialogues* in 1966 and completed it in 1968. But it was rejected by at least three publishers before Knopf accepted it, along with *Grendel,* in November 1970. As a result, though Gardner revised the opening of *The Sunlight Dialogues* and made other changes after Knopf accepted it, the novel was essentially complete before he wrote the final drafts of *The Wreckage of Agathon* (1970) or *Grendel* (1971). Since these novels echo its principal characters and themes, it is helpful to see them, particularly *Grendel,* in the context that *The Sunlight Dialogues* provides. For example, Grendel's paradoxical redemption is implicitly glossed by the dust jacket of *The Sunlight Dialogues,* where Gardner writes, on the front flap, that the novel's antagonists drive each other "to a bedrock humanness, stripped of illusion, full of grace."

Despite its elaborate plot and length (674 pages), *The Sunlight Dialogues* was on the *New York Times* best-sellers list for fourteen weeks, and some of Gardner's most discriminating critics argue that it is his best novel. Its only flaws stem from Gardner's attempt to write a *Moby-Dick* for the twentieth century. With eight story lines and more than eighty characters, *The Sunlight Dialogues* is a demanding novel. It is a tribute to Gardner's achievement that so many people have enjoyed the challenge.

Though Gardner sets the novel in 1966, in Batavia, New York, he creates, as in *The Resurrection,* a Gothic atmosphere of foreboding and mystery. To narrate the novel, he establishes a distinctly felt—but unnamed—persona whom he later identified in interviews as "Warburton Hodge," a distant cousin of the family at the center of the novel. The detachment of this omniscient narrator distinguishes him from the narrators of *The Resurrection* and *Nickel Mountain*. By maintaining an ironic voice and by portraying the central characters as resembling both animals and clowns, Gardner hoped to create an emotional distance and avoid the sentimentality which he felt had marred *Nickel Mountain*.

This cartoon vision, which is echoed by John Napper's illustrations, creates a paradoxical tone, a fusion of comic incongruities and tragic occurrences perhaps best characterized as "grotesque." In contradicting the assumption that the novel was "realistic," Gardner said: "In *The Sunlight Dialogues* I wanted to tell a story which had the feel of total fabulation, total mystery—magicians—strange things and impossible tricks—so that everybody would have the sudden feeling at some point in the novel that he's caught inside a novel. . . . I wanted to make people in the novel just as much like Batavians as possible and yet create the feeling that the whole novel is taking place in Oz."[1] But this creation of "total fabulation," of a world like Oz—which Gardner alludes to in the novel—is sometimes ignored by readers. In response to the authority and intensity of Gardner's vision, some readers accommodate themselves to the novel's fabulous events and cartoonlike characters and see the novel as "realistic."

The novel combines the form of the epic (twenty-four chapters) with the interwoven and counterpointed story lines of the medieval romance. The romance that Gardner had specifically in mind was Thomas Malory's *Le Morte Darthur* (for which he wrote a *Cliff's Notes* during the time he was composing the novel). He saw Malory's vision as dark and despairing, and totally compatible with that of the twentieth century.[2] And he employed the romance as a controlling metaphor, introducing an Arthur figure and a Merlin figure; and setting scenes in a castlelike police station, a basement which resembles a dungeon, a Gothic-style church, and a burial crypt.

The novel's unifying conflict is between Batavia's police chief, Fred Clumly, who is the "King Arthur" of the parody; and a half-mad magician, "The Sunlight Man," who is the "Merlin" of the parody. Together, they generate what Gardner called his "cops and robbers" plot—the basic thrust of the novel. Clumly, the sixty-four-year-old "cop," is already losing control of law and order in Batavia when the Sunlight Man pushes him toward spiritual anarchy—and redemption—in four "dialogues" staged with progressively more elaborate tricks of illusion. Like King Arthur's Merlin, the Sunlight Man performs acts of magic with sometimes evil results. But ultimately the Sunlight Man—later identified as Taggert Hodge—goes too far in his Faustian role, and loses his spiritual identity, if not his soul, in mocking Christianity and affirming the pagan faith of the Babylonians.

As his name suggests, Clumly is intellectually clumsy, or inept, though he was once considered quick-witted. He likes to say he is "cognizant," but his vision of reality has been dimmed by time and routine. Gardner symbolizes Clumly's journey toward metaphysical awareness when he alludes to "sunlight" in the novel's title and has Taggert Hodge parody Plato's dialogues by conducting what are, in fact, bizarre monologues. Taggert, the embodiment of anarchy, leads Clumly, the embodiment of law and order, through a process of discovery. In book 7 of Plato's *Republic* the prisoners in his

The Sunlight Dialogues

metaphorical cave see only "shadows" of images of people and objects. If they could turn to see behind them, they would be blinded by the fire. If they could find their way out of the cave, they would be blinded by the sunlight of reality. In adopting the role of "reality instructor," Taggert Hodge— himself blinded by visions of fire—suggests that he is bringing "sunlight" into Clumly's cavelike world. But Taggert's sunlight is itself an illusion. The only reality he ultimately sees is the existential void. By contrast, and despite his intellectual myopia, Clumly is gifted with intuition. He believes (like the philosopher Alfred North Whitehead) that all things are connected and, like Chandler in response to Viola in *The Resurrection,* he ultimately feels a transcendent love for the Sunlight Man which is generalized into a love for all humanity.

To suggest Clumly's limited perceptions, Gardner creates a Disney-like portrait, emphasizing Clumly's "large nose, which was like a mole's, and his teeth . . . strikingly white and without a flaw,"[3] and adding that a disease has caused Clumly to lose all his body hair and turn into "a grublike, virtually hairless monster . . ." (13). In essence, Clumly is a tragicomic grotesque who has groped his way, like a mole or a grub, through life until his spiritual conflict with the Sunlight Man makes him truly cognizant of a sunlit reality.

Taggert Hodge adopts the role of the Sunlight Man after being emotionally as well as physically scarred by fire. Like Clumly, his grotesque appearance reflects the metaphysical distortions of his character and vision: "His forehead was high and domelike, scarred, wrinkled, drawn, right up into the hairline, and above the arc of his balding, his hair exploded like chaotic sunbeams around an Eastern tomb" (59). Always clowning, he wrenches his scarred face into a smile, yet, with his "wounded eyes burning deep in the ashes of his face"

(61), he projects his fire-stormed madness on Clumly's world while seeking meaning for his own. He smells as "if he'd been feeding on the dead . . ." (60), and he compares himself to a goat in a long poem (310–11) which Gardner had published separately as "The Ruptured Goat."

The Sunlight Dialogues is, in sum, part cyclical romance, part Gothic novel, part detective novel, part metaphysical inquiry. It starts with the mystery of the Sunlight Man's identity and evolves into the larger question of humanity's purpose in an unknowable universe. When Clumly's officers arrest the Sunlight Man for writing "LOVE" on a Batavia street, he burns his identification papers and speaks gibberish. All that Clumly knows initially is that this bearded man with the scarred face and high-domed forehead is no ordinary vagrant. To the reactionary Clumly, the Sunlight Man seems to be from California—and therefore a threat to Clumly's only truth: "law and order." Paradoxically, however, the Sunlight Man's anarchism rekindles Clumly's fading interest in life.

Clumly has lived for years in a metaphorical darkness with his blind wife Esther, who keeps the lights off in their house and tipples wine to blur the edges of reality. Esther has always felt that she was a burden to Clumly. Once, when he gently complained about a hair in his food, she threatened to cut her throat with a razor blade—but then—in one of Gardner's many comic touches—she had to ask Clumly where the blades were. Even now, moving into old age, she dreams of setting Clumly free, as she sits in the dark house sewing a dress that is never finished, in an echo of Homer's Penelope and her endless weaving. Yet Esther is also Clumly's Beatrice, his inspiration as he ventures, like Dante, through the world of his dreams (Gardner later claimed that Clumly, once a sailor, had read Dante at sea.)[4] And Esther is both the Blind Maiden of the cyclical romance, who must save the knight, and the Esther of the Old Testament, who must save the Hebrews—in her case the "Hebrew" Clumly, who is characterized as such by Taggert Hodge, the would-be "Babylonian." At the same time, despite her symbolic burden, Esther is one of Gardner's most grotesque characters: her voice combines a whine with false cheeriness, she has "glass eyes" (which she takes out at night), her head sways on her long neck like "a hairy sunflower" (8), and she envisions herself as a "chicken" (544). Yet—whether Penelope, Beatrice, Blind Maiden, or "chicken"—Esther's love for Clumly transcends, unsentimentally, the absurdity of her character.

Esther is unaware of Clumly's involvement with the Sunlight Man, but Will Hodge Sr. knows immediately that the Sunlight Man is his brother Taggert, and he follows Clumly, hoping he will lead him to Taggert. Meanwhile, other characters are in motion: Will's ex-wife (Millie Jewell Hodge); their two sons (Will Jr. and Luke); and Walter Benson (alias Walter Boyle), a professional burglar. These characters develop eight plot strands: 1) Taggert or the Sunlight Man's story; 2) Clumly's story; 3) Esther's story; 4) Benson/Boyle's story; 5) Will Hodge Sr.'s story; 6) Millie Hodge's story; 7) Will Hodge Jr.'s story; and 8) Luke Hodge's story. And each character's story parallels and, to a varying extent, informs the other stories in what Gardner called an "architectonic," as opposed to an Aristotelian, plot.

The Aristotelian plot is made up of strongly impelled cause-and-effect actions, with each action providing a further complication of the initial conflict until the total rhythm of the work rises to a turning point, climax, and denouement. By contrast, the "architectonic" plot, as Gardner defined it, introduces two or more causally related and parallel plots.[5] In *The Sunlight Dialogues,* Gardner unites his eight plot strands by focusing on his "cops and robbers" plot (Clumly vs. Taggert, the Sunlight Man) and by parodying the structure of the medieval romance, with its counterpointing and mirroring of characters, actions, images, and symbols.

In developing the Arthurian analogue, Gardner also parodies T. S. Eliot's synthesis of King Arthur with the Fisher King in *The Waste Land.* The counterpoint to Clumly's "Arthur" is former U.S. Congressman Arthur S. Hodge, the late patriarch of the Hodge family and a man almost omniscient in his wisdom. He had built Stony Hill Farm, once an Eden, and had been blessed with promising sons, of which Taggert was the youngest, the most brilliant, and the most charming. Then Arthur had lapsed into senility and obesity (a recurrent motif in Gardner's novels) and his sons, once noble "knights," had gone their errant ways.

Chief Clumly supervises a police station which, like its real-life prototype in Batavia, is decorated with turrets and looks like an "imitation castle" (148). Gardner first hints at Clumly's Arthurian persona in a prologue, where, some years after the events of the novel, a nasty old judge tells Clumly, now a widower and long since retired, "take any ordinary man, give him a weapon—say, x caliber—" (3). But Gardner is even more directly allusive in the body of the novel, when he has Clumly, fighting to maintain control, tell one of his less-dedicated subordinates, Kozlowski, "I'm responsible for this town, you follow that? Responsible! It's like a king. I don't mean I'm comparing myself to a king, you understand, but it's *like* a king. If a king's laws get tangled up and his knights all fail him, he's got to do the job himself" (378).

But Clumly does not do the job himself, and Miller, his loyal second in command, covers for him as best he can. Meanwhile Clumly finds consolation by attending funerals—most significantly, the funeral of Mickey Salvador, a young officer killed when the Sunlight Man helps a young Indian (Nick Slater) escape from Clumly's jail: "At last, whatever tensions, uncertainties, joys and sorrows warred in the heart, law and order were restored, and there was peace" (380). It is a peace that Clumly has partially found in his death-in-life with Esther, a wasteland existence from which the Sunlight Man rescues him.

Gardner foreshadows Clumly's spiritual redemption by introducing an elderly blind woman, who speaks in Italian of her spiritual vision while a young boy translates: "Storms of birds," "flights of pigeons," "death"; and then: "Some will die for uncontrol and animalness and for cruel mastering. Some for violent kindness." But the boy fails to translate her climactic word, "*disanimata*" (380–81), even though she repeats it, touching Clumly's face with ice-cold hands.

Gardner told his interviewers that the blind woman is an "oracle," a "real ancient sibyl," and translated the word *disanimata* as "disanimated," noting that Clumly comes to understand her meaning in his final speech at the end of the novel.[6] Taggert, by contrast, pretends to be an oracle in his role as the Sunlight Man, and desperately hopes his visions are true. But he has been driven mad by spiritual suffering and, as the old woman's prophecy suggests, his "uncontrol," his "animalness" (he smells like a goat), and his "violent kindness" (especially toward Clumly and Millie Hodge) lead him to self-destruction. He had begun to lose control sixteen years before, when his wife Kathleen had gone insane, and he had paid for her expensive therapy by embezzling from the law firm he partnered with his brother Will. When Kathleen set fire to the office, the insurance adjusters found the discrepancy, and he had fled Batavia.

As in his previous novels, Gardner employs the Gothic device of insanity to motivate his characters' perceptual distortion of reality, especially their seeing "ghosts." At the same time, Gardner suspends narrative resolution, creating suspense by filtering important details in fragments through the memories of his central characters. This technique is most dramatically in evidence when he withholds information about the events leading up to the moment that Taggert wrote the word "LOVE" on Oak Street in Batavia.

Taggert's actions during this period are not clear until late in the novel—and then only partially—when traumatic memories begin to surface in his consciousness, and the reader learns that (apparently) Taggert had almost burned to death while trying to save his sons from a house in Phoenix which Kathleen had set fire to; that Taggert was later convinced the boys were still alive and that Kathleen's brothers had taken them along with Kathleen to Batavia (while Taggert was recovering in the hospital) and placed them under the control of her father, Clive Paxton. Not until Taggert sees their graves in a Batavia cemetery does he accept the reality of their loss—a traumatic recognition which causes him to sob uncontrollably and see fire all around him—though he knows it does not exist. Yet he decides, in his madness, to console Clive Paxton, whom he hates. Time blurs and he is arrested the next morning for painting on the street. Only at the end of the novel does Gardner reveal the mystery, when Taggert has a hallucination of Clive Paxton talking to the "ghost" of his father—and allows himself to remember "putting his hands around Clive Paxton's throat" (627). But even then, Gardner retains the ambiguity of the moment: there are no signs of violence on Paxton's body, and his death is officially attributed to the failure of a gravely diseased heart.

Taggert's ambiguous gesture of compassion brings about the first of a series of deaths which contradict his role as "savior." Taggert has lost those he loves most—his father to a slow death of mind and body, his sons to fire, his wife to madness. He is left with an apocalyptic vision of a world in flames. Though he assumes the role of a magician and cosmic clown, he ultimately becomes a monster. Fighting against annihilating despair, he performs feats of illusion and mocks himself as well as Clumly with his so-called dialogues. He rejects Clumly's ideas of order and asserts his own existential freedom, momentarily clinging to Babylonian myths, but ultimately giving into nihilism and sinking downward to darkness (and chaos), while the molelike, grublike Clumly tunnels upward to an enlightened faith in spiritual connectedness.

Taggert's escape from Clumly's custody leads to escalating violence and drives the novel's complex plot. When Taggert frees Nick Slater from jail, he sets off a chain of murders. When Clumly meets with Taggert, hoping he can recapture him, Taggert torments him with his quasi-dialectical search for metaphysical order. And when Taggert is not tormenting Clumly, he is tormenting the once-beautiful Millie Hodge, whom he holds captive along with her son Luke and Nick Slater in the partially flooded cellar of Luke's farmhouse.

Though Taggert is momentarily attracted to Millie, he remembers her destructiveness toward his brother Will Sr., whom she married and betrayed; and Taggert punishes her, telling himself that he is redeeming her while parodying the language and symbolic actions of Christ. As suggested, Gardner is echoing medieval romance and combining it with Gothic elements. If Clumly plays King Arthur to Taggert's Merlin, Millie plays Merlin's evil antagonist, the witch Morgan le Fay: "He'd made her a foul old witch for her crimes, and now he was chief victim of her witchcraft. Or she'd been a witch before and he had exorcised her demon . . ." (625). But as Leslie Fiedler observes, American authors generally move toward self-mockery and parody when they use Gothic machinery to objectify the "hidden blackness of the human soul and human society."[7] Gardner is no exception. Taggert Hodge has made a Faustian pact with pagan (Babylonian) gods. Millie is a witch, if not a pagan goddess.[8] And Gardner parodies the fiction—or "dream"—he has created, encouraging the reader to question the illusion of the text and employing the metafictional techniques that get even greater play in *Grendel, The King's Indian,* and *October Light.*

This literary self-consciousness is especially notable in chapter 20, when Taggert brings Millie, Luke, and Nick upstairs from the flooded cellar for a performance of magic. Though barely in control of either his thoughts or his actions, Taggert has the psychic energy to create an amazing illusion: he shoots and apparently kills a sparrow, then brings it back to life. Most readers, convinced by now that Taggert is a skilled illusionist, would probably accept this event as the ultimate example of his genius. Gardner, however, encourages the reader to question not only the circumstances of the bird's "death" but the illusion of the scene itself by footnoting the event and explaining how the trick works.

Moreover, Gardner questions the reality of Millie's character. When Taggert comments despairingly on the "fantastic insignificance of it all," and suggests "that the center of it all is Time" (620), Millie realizes temporarily that she is "merely a character in an endless, meaningless novel, then forgot'' (620). But Gardner does not allow the reader to forget. Contradicting his later demand, in *On Moral Fiction*[9] and elsewhere, that a writer create and maintain an unbroken fictive ''dream,'' he reinforces the reader's consciousness of the text by having Taggert—on page 621—say that ''there's always the future, p. 622.''

In detaching the reader from the illusion of the novel at its most nihilistic moment, Gardner was employing the techniques of John Barth and other postmodernists, just as he did later in ''The King's Indian.'' But after this brief interlude of self-consciousness, Gardner returns to his concern in this chapter with the idea of love. He begins the chapter with the statement that Millie ''had underestimated hate'' (611) in responding to Taggert and his sadistic acts. By the end of the chapter, however, she realizes that ''she has underestimated love'' (624); that love, more than hate, has made Taggert the monster he has become. But if Taggert is defeated because he has loved too much, Millie is defeated because she has loved too little.

Millie has destroyed the capacity of both her sons to love—or to maintain close emotional relationships. Will Jr., with his low-slung jaw, balding head, and hunched shoulders, is a cartoon copy of his father, with whom he once shared a law practice. But like his mother, he is both smarter and more emotionally alienated, and his marriage has suffered. Millie's son Luke is also described in cartoon terms, although he does not resemble his brother: his ears stick out like Dumbo the elephant's, and his eyebrows have a witchlike arch which suggests the emotional tensions that cause his violent, all-consuming headaches. Though considerably younger and more highly strung than his brother, Luke is in his mother's eyes a spiritual weakling, and Millie has repeatedly goaded him, hoping somehow that he will metamorphose into her distorted vision of an ideal man. Instead, he has sunk into feelings of inadequacy, self-loathing, and rage—emotions which ultimately fuel his bizarre act of atonement. Encouraged by Millie to drive Taggert and Nick to safety, he instead crashes the truck into the river, sacrificing his life to stop the endless pattern of destruction his uncle has inspired.

Though Taggert escapes the truck moments before Luke's fatal action, he cannot escape the guilt he feels over his nephew's death, and he virtually commits suicide by tricking a frightened police officer—who shoots him in a panic while Taggert is in the act of giving himself up. Then, in a final irony, Gardner prints a facsimile of the Certificate of Death on the last page of the novel, where Taggert, the chaos figure, is described as having been fatally injured by a "police action in pursuit of order."

Taggert gives Clumly a new word: "metaphysical." And along with the word, Clumly finds a new reality, just at a point when he has "renounced the world" (13). Until now, he has numbly accepted the grey stews and lukewarm Sanka which symbolize his life with Esther. But once his idea of order is disturbed by the Sunlight Man, he moves toward a spiritual rebirth. Giving into the first intellectual and emotional excitement he has felt in many years, he risks his life as well as his career to meet and listen to the Sunlight Man.

Clumly's quest for knowledge is counterpointed by Will Hodge Sr. Like Clumly, Will Sr. defends himself against humiliation and disappointment by leading a carefully restricted existence. But also like Clumly, he forgets his personal concerns in tracking the Sunlight Man. From the moment his apartment is entered without force after the Sunlight Man has escaped, he knows more than Clumly does: that the Sunlight

Man is actually Taggert Hodge, and that Taggert was somehow involved in the murder of Will Sr.'s landlady.

Will Hodge Jr.'s pursuit of R. V. Kleppmann parallels his
father's pursuit of Taggert, but his actions do not influence either his father's actions or Clumly's, and some readers question the relevance of his actions to the total plot. Though a
lawyer like his father, Will Jr. has made a career out of chasing
individuals who "skip" town without paying their creditors.
Driven by an obsession—the capture of Kleppmann, the ultimate "skip"—Will Jr. creates a parodic and self-reflexive
counterpoint to the rest of the novel. In the chapter titled "The
Dragon's Dwelling-Place and the Court of Owls," he tracks
Kleppmann down to his home—actually Gardner's home—
south of Carbondale, Illinois. To this autobiographical allusion, Gardner adds a parody of Faulkner's "The Bear,"
echoing the moment when Isaac McCaslin performs the ritual
that will lead him to the long-sought and mystical animal: "It
was as if he [Will Hodge Jr.] had thrown away his compass, in
the classical way, and had ventured into the thickness of the
woods prepared for whatever he was destined to meet . . ."
(568). Then, when Will Jr. actually confronts Kleppmann,
Gardner parallels the imagery associated with the miserly
dragon in *Grendel,* describing Kleppmann as an "upright
crocodile" and "an elderly serpent," and indicating that he
acts like "a dead man, all mechanical good manners, or the
Wizard of Oz, his mind far away, behind some curtain pushing
buttons and watching with tiny, sharp eyes" (572).

More integral to the central plot, and even more grotesquely comic, is Gardner's portrayal of Walter Benson (alias
Boyle), who functions as the personification of the divided
self, acting as a detached observer of the action, offering information about the past, and making judgments about the

present. At the same time, his wife, Marguerite, contrasts sharply with Clumly's wife, Esther. Marguerite, an unattractive and silly woman, carries on an amusing dalliance with the equally unattractive and exploitive Ollie Nuper, a political agitator who rents a room in the Bensons' house. By the same token, Walter cheats on Marguerite in his own fashion by telling her that he is a travelling salesman when in fact he is a travelling burglar who has used the alias ''Walter Boyle'' so long he has trouble remembering what his name really is.

While Clumly is a doer, however inept, Benson/Boyle's activities as a burglar force him to assume the role of an impotent observer. He knows, for example, the true identity of the Sunlight Man. And he knows that fascist thugs have murdered his nemesis Ollie Nuper. But to speak out in either case is to reveal his true self and risk prosecution. He has to protect his two selves: *Walter Benson,* a businessman and a poet (who writes in a comically sentimental imitation of Edgar Guest); and *Walter Boyle,* a burglar. As two people in one body, Benson/Boyle is the grotesque personification of the thematic tensions developed in the periodic ''dialogues'' between Clumly and Taggert: law vs. anarchy, order vs. chaos, responsibility vs. freedom.

All four dialogues and many of Gardner's chapter titles borrow from A. Leo Oppenheim's *Ancient Mesopotamia: Portrait of a Dead Civilization.*[10] Some of the chapter titles recapitulate, often ironically, the inscriptions on the cuneiform tablets photographically reproduced by Oppenheim. For example, chapter 3 (entitled ''Lion Emerging from Cage'') portrays Will Hodge Sr. in his spiritual awakening; chapter 5 (''Hunting Wild Asses'') shows Clumly hunting Taggert, Mayor Mullen, and Will Hodge Sr.; chapter 19 (''Workmen in a Quarry'') shows Clumly's prosecution by Mayor Mullen; and chapter 20 ("Winged Figure Carrying Sacrificial Animal") shows Millie encouraging Luke to drive Taggert to freedom— the act which inspires Luke to sacrifice his life.

Gardner's chapter titles also make ironic use of captions and phrases from *Ancient Mesopotamia*. For example, chapter 2 (entitled "When the Exorcist Shall Go to the House of the Patient") shows Taggert "exorcising"—or freeing—Nick from jail; chapter 4 ("Mama") shows Millie rejecting her role as mother; chapter 9 ("Like a robber, I shall proceed according to my will") shows Clumly proceeding like an outlaw after he fails to capture Taggert; chapter 23 ("*Nah ist—und schwer zu fassen der Gott* ["Near is God/And hard to understand"]), shows Clumly's inability to comprehend Taggert's metaphysical assertions; and, finally, chapter 23 ("*E silentio*" [Latin: "out of silence"]) uses Oppenheim's speculation on ideas of immortality in *The Epic of Gilgamesh* to underline the painful silence beyond death: Luke's death for his father and Taggert's death for Clumly.

But the major debt to Oppenheim lies in the content of the four dialogues. It is immediately clear that Taggert's articulation of Babylonian, as opposed to Hebrew, religious beliefs is beyond Clumly's immediate interest or comprehension. And since he falls asleep during Taggert's initial lecture—or homily—at the First Presbyterian Church, it seems fortunate to Clumly that he has taped Taggert's voice. (Later, however, the tapes betray the fact of their meeting and cost Clumly his job.)

Though some journalistic reviewers suggested that they were as bored as Clumly is by Taggert's lectures on Babylonian religion, the lectures/dialogues are nevertheless central to Gardner's parody of Sartrean existentialism. Most important to Taggert—and most important thematically—is the Babylonians' failure to conceive of guilt. Unlike the Hebrews and the

Christians, they believed that the body and the spirit are permanently separate and that the mystery of their relationship is insoluble. Guilt, Taggert emphasizes, is a Hebrew concept, and Clumly, by Taggert's definition, is a Hebrew, a believer in law and order—and guilt. But Taggert suggests, introducing the metaphor of "sunlight," that Clumly also lives in a Platonic cave of ignorance: he is like the black man who, trapped in a cellar and lied to for years, cannot accept reality when he finally escapes.

Taggert, by contrast to Clumly, defines himself as a Babylonian, since he claims to believe, as they did, that the spiritual world was unknowable except through divination, astrology, omens, and particularly intuition. A Babylonian ruler was dependent on his diviners when dealing with the spirit world. Without precedent to guide him, without fixed policies, the ruler tried to remain open to experience and intuition so that he could interpret the meaning of what Taggert calls the "mumbling gods," and thus be free to act with the wisdom of the moment rather than of the past.

But ultimately Taggert's denial of history and guilt lead him (in Gardner's evolving parody of Sartre) to the nihilism he has fought to transcend by desperate affirmation. He has no answers for the problems of the contemporary world and no faith that the problems will not increase. He believes that the "Hebrew" (or Judeo-Christian system) is not in harmony with the cosmos or the order that he wishes to affirm. And since the system is failing, he tries to act freely and spontaneously, choosing (in Sartrean fashion) authentically. But his supposedly inspired and/or authentic acts result in the death of other human beings. The guilt he has denied finally overwhelms him.

Taggert's growing despair becomes progressively more evident in the eccentricity of the subject matter and settings of the dialogues that follow. During their second meeting ("The

Dialogue of Houses''), conducted in a tent decorated with astrological symbols and suspended above a railroad track, Taggert talks briefly to Clumly about astrology (the ''houses'' of
the sun). Then he distinguishes between magic and divination
(or omen-watching): while magic attempts to influence the
gods' actions, divination ''is man's attempt to find out what
the universe is doing. . . . After divination one acts *with* the
gods. You discover which way things are flowing, and you
swim in the same direction. You allow yourself to be pos-
sessed'' (419). But Taggert never discovers the flow (an image
which Gardner associates with Boethian ideas of determinism)
and he becomes even more outrageous, demanding that
Clumly meet him next in a burial crypt, where, in ''The Dialogue of the Dead,'' he explicates the metaphysical meaning
of the ancient Babylonian epic *Gilgamesh* (c. 1400 B.C.).[11]
Since by Babylonian logic, death is real and immortality is
doubtful, Taggert tells Clumly that the ''ultimate act, the act
which comes when the gods command it, is utterly imper-
sonal, a movement of the universe, a stroke by, for, and of sole
interest to—the gods'' (533). But if this is the case, Taggert
asks rhetorically, then why act at all? Because ''action is life''
(533), he answers halfheartedly, admitting that he is guilty of
murder and confronting Clumly with a moral decision: According to Taggert, if Clumly acts on the ''side of the universe,'' he will let him escape; but if Clumly acts ''for
humanity,'' he will arrest him and prevent further crises.
When Clumly chooses not to arrest Taggert, however, he acts
not on the ''side of the universe,'' or any other abstraction, but
out of compassion, if not love, for the man who has resurrected him from a death-in-life.

During ''The Dialogue of Towers,'' held at Stony Hill
Farm, the Hodge family's ancestral home, Taggert gives up his
role as the ''Sunlight Man'' almost entirely. It is their final

meeting, and he has now lost all hope. He calls Clumly's attention to the silo of the barn and compares it to the towers of Babylon, echoing Eliot's bleak vision of "Falling towers" in *The Waste Land*. What Clumly hears now are not metaphysical abstractions but Taggert's apocalyptic vision of spiritual, social, and political chaos: "Vietnam is the beginning. No matter how long it takes, the end is upon us . . ." (631). His hope for cosmic harmony and "salvation" has been destroyed, and he suddenly causes the silo to burst into flames. Clumly, by contrast, transcends the rigidity of his old self and snatches Taggert's gun. But when Clumly tells Taggert "You're free" (634), he is unintentionally ironic, since—as Gardner repeatedly makes clear—Taggert is already the victim of his existential freedom.

Though Clumly has lost his job because he failed to arrest the Sunlight Man, he honors a previous commitment to speak on "Law and Order" to the Dairyman's League at the Grange Hall. Profoundly empathetic with Taggert, he has a mystical vision of his future, as the light inside the Grange looks "for an instant like fire" (662)—and then he learns that Taggert has been killed. Overwhelmed with grief, he departs from his speech and talks instead of Taggert's death, his brilliant mind, the pressures of police work, rambling incoherently and often comically—as when he tells his bewildered audience about the risk of entropy—that the universe "can get cold. Turn ice. Ladies and gentleman, we mustn't let that happen . . ." (670). But then, finally, after groping for meaning among random facts, he feels the pressure of the audience, which stares at him "as wide-eyed and still as fish," and he says, automatically and impulsively, beyond the reach of his intellect: " 'Blessed are the meek, by which I mean all of us, including the Sunlight Man'. . . . 'God be kind to all Good

Samaritans and also bad ones. For such is the Kingdom of Heaven' '' (672).

In blessing all humanity, including ''bad Samaritans'' like Taggert Hodge and Good Samaritans like Esther (whom he calls ''a model for us all''), Clumly moves toward redemption in the wake of Coleridge's Ancient Mariner and previous Gardner heroes. In doing so, he intuitively realizes the vision of the old Italian woman (Gardner's ''oracle''), who foresaw the death of Taggert in her warning about uncontrolled, animallike, and ''violent kindness.'' But Clumly only knows pure emotion as the audience's enthusiastic applause lifts and hurtles ''him up to where the light was brighter than sun-filled clouds, disanimated and holy'' (673). And he remains beyond rational thought until the Fire Chief (Taggert's ''fiery'' surrogate) says happily, ''Powerful sermon! God forgive us!'' Only then does Clumly realize that he has sermonized and, in Coleridge's words, ''blessed them unaware.'' But instead of a sudden, cosmic sunburst of light, his epiphany is a slow, comic dawning on his molelike consciousness: ''. . . Clumly, in a last pitch of seasickness, caught him in his arms and said 'Correct!' and then, more wildly, shocked to wisdom, he cried *'Correct!'* ''

Though Clumly's redemption is more comic, if not more grotesque, than that of James Chandler, he is closer to Coleridge's Mariner in the experience of ''amazing grace'' and the rebirth out of a death-in-life, and he points the way to a still more unlikely hero: the monster Grendel.

NOTES

1. Joe David Bellamy and Pat Ensworth, ''John Gardner,'' *The New Fiction: Interviews with Innovative American Writers,* ed. Joe David Bellamy (Urbana: University of Illinois Press, 1974) 191.

Understanding John Gardner

2. Digby Diehl, "Medievalist in Illinois Ozarks," *Los Angeles Times* 5 Sept. 1971: 43.

3. John Gardner, *The Sunlight Dialogues* (New York: Knopf, 1972) 8. Parenthetical page references in the text are to this edition.

4. Paul F. Ferguson, John R. Maier, Frank McConnell, and Sara Matthiessen. "The Art of Fiction LXXIII: John Gardner," *Paris Review* 21 (Spring 1979): 62.

5. See Gardner on "Plotting," *The Art of Fiction: Notes on Craft for Young Writers* (New York: Knopf, 1984) 165–94.

6. Bellamy and Ensworth 175–76.

7. Leslie A. Fiedler, *Love and Death in the American Novel*, rev. ed. (New York: Dell, 1966) 7.

8. In his study of Gardner's use of A. Leo Oppenheim's *Ancient Mesopotamia: Portrait of a Dead Civilization* (University of Chicago Press, 1964), Gregory L. Morris suggests that Millie's character echoes both the faithless Babylonian goddess "Istar" and (ironically) "Mama," creator of mankind; see Morris, "A Babylonian in Batavia: Mesopotamian Literature and Lore in *The Sunlight Dialogues*," *John Gardner: Critical Perspectives*, ed. Robert A. Morace and Kathryn VanSpanckeren (Carbondale: Southern Illinois University Press, 1982) 28–45.

9. See John Gardner, *On Moral Fiction* (New York: Basic Books, 1978) 89, 91, 112.

10. For a detailed discussion of Gardner's debt to Oppenheim, see Morris 28–45.

11. Gardner retained a keen interest in *Gilgamesh* throughout his career. At the time of his death, he and John Maier had just completed a verse translation of the epic (from the ancient Akkadian language); see *Gilgamesh* (New York: Knopf, 1984).

CHAPTER FOUR

Grendel

Though John Gardner sometimes referred to his novel *Grendel* (1971) as a tour de force written in a short period of time, its narrative resonance suggests that the monster-hero (Grendel) had been lurking in his imagination for some years. By the time he completed the novel in summer of 1970, he had been teaching and puzzling over the Anglo-Saxon epic *Beowulf*—his source of inspiration—for twelve years. Moreover, as previously observed, Grendel's tragicomic character and nihilistic vision is anticipated by Taggert Hodge in *The Sunlight Dialogues* and by Agathon in *The Wreckage of Agathon*—though Grendel is more comically grotesque and infinitely more poetic than either Taggert Hodge or Agathon.

Grendel, a giant, bearlike monster, is doomed to wander the earth alone, eternally alienated from human connection. In *Beowulf,* he is merely a symbol of darkness, chaos, and death. In *Grendel,* Gardner creates a fully realized character—a monster with a sense of humor and a gift for language. He narrates his own version of the events recorded in *Beowulf* and reveals himself not only as a grotesque figure, but as a tragicomic poet whose suffering elicits sympathy, despite the often horrible nature of his actions.

Grendel is a work of fabulation with an unreality echoed by Emil Antonucci's woodcut abstractions, which appear at the twelve chapter openings. *Grendel* is also a work of metafiction. In rhythmically stressed prose Gardner deconstructs the original epic's characters and actions (and many of

Understanding John Gardner

its lines) by placing them in an ironic context which implicitly questions the vision of the original work while saluting its literary power. Improvising on the original, Gardner both echoes and recasts while synthesizing characters, images, and ideas with those of various literary and philosophical works.

Though a reader can appreciate *Grendel* without knowing *Beowulf,* an awareness of the epic reveals the ingenuity as well as the irony of Gardner's improvisation and parody. Set in sixth-century Denmark, the epic features Hrothgar, the once powerful but now aging king of the Danes; Wealtheow, his beautiful and charismatic young wife; Beowulf, the hero with the strength of thirty men who comes to Hrothgar's court from Geatland (modern Sweden); and the three monsters Beowulf kills: Grendel; Grendel's mother; and the dragon, which fatally wounds Beowulf before it dies.

In *Beowulf,* the original Grendel's appearance is restricted to the poem's first 861 lines (from Beowulf's arrival to Grendel's death). In *Grendel,* Gardner juggles the characters and events. He creates a relationship between Grendel and his mother, who has lost the power of language and mumbles unintelligibly while picking among the bones in their cave below the fiery pond. He creates a relationship between Grendel and one of Hrothgar's leading thanes—Unferth—a minor character in the original. And he creates a relationship between Grendel and the dragon, who only appears at the end of the epic, fifty years after the original Grendel's death.

Gardner recasts other events. In the epic, Beowulf swims down through the fiery pond to kill Grendel's mother after she avenges her son's death. In the novel, Gardner has Unferth swim down and try to kill Grendel, who responds by ridiculing Unferth's attempt at heroism. The epic's central conflict is between Beowulf and the three monsters: Grendel, his mother, and the dragon. The central conflict in the novel is within the mind of Grendel, who must choose between the spiritual "connectedness" of the ordered world envisioned by the "Shaper," Hrothgar's poet-singer; and the spiritual disconnectedness of the mechanistic world envisioned by Grendel's nihilistic "dragon."

Although Gardner indicated elsewhere that he thought Beowulf was a Christ figure in the epic,[1] he inverts the character of Beowulf in *Grendel,* playing against the reader's assumptions about heroes by making him a cold-eyed killer who might well be featured in a work of science fiction. (Gardner refers to him on the original dust jacket, for example, as "the weird stranger, Beowulf, defender of mankind, half dragon, half computer, with empty eyes.") Similarly, Gardner plays against the reader's assumptions about monsters. In *Beowulf,* Grendel is an incarnation of chaos and evil. In *Grendel,* he is a potentially warmhearted creature who is so hurt by the rejection of human beings that he ends up eating them. Like Dr. Frankenstein's sensitive monster (who also inspired a poem and a libretto by Gardner), Grendel is portrayed as an alienated being who feels despair and rage, and who displaces these feelings with violent acts.

The structure of *Grendel* is "lyrical,"[2] rather than plotted or causal. The novel's twelve chapters seem to progress in a temporal or chronological fashion, but this is illusory. Grendel speaks of past events for the first eight chapters, and only the last four chapters focus on the present moment, anticipate Beowulf's arrival, and foreshadow Grendel's death. As the chapters progress, Grendel reflects on his loss of connection with his mother, his loss of connection with human beings, his "war" with Hrothgar, the history of Hrothgar's rise to power, the spellbinding message of Hrothgar's Shaper, and (in chapter 5) on the even more spellbinding message of the dragon—a terrifying figment of Grendel's imagination which he discovers in the dark side of his consciousness. Meanwhile, the progression of the seasons is reflected in each of the twelve chapters with an allusion to the relevant sun sign of the zodiac.

Grendel must choose between the nihilistic vision of his dragon and the idealistic vision of Hrothgar's blind Shaper. Though initially inspired by *Beowulf,* Grendel's dragon is a creative synthesis of medieval art, William Blake, J. R. R. Tolkien, Walt Disney, and—as in *The Sunlight Dialogues*—L. Frank Baum's *The Wizard of Oz.* Most significantly, however, Grendel's dragon objectifies the ideas of Jean-Paul Sartre. By the same token, though the Shaper in *Grendel* was initially inspired by *Beowulf,* and though, as in *Beowulf,* his poetry salutes and enhances the past and future glory of Hrothgar, his imagery and metaphors are associated by Grendel's dragon with Alfred North Whitehead's metaphor of organic "connectedness."

Gardner's notes for the novel indicate that he wanted to create a tension between despair and comedy by making Grendel a "chaos figure," who is "wretched with despair," yet has a "maniacal sense of humor" which Gardner hoped to reveal through a "comedy of rage."[3] Gardner envisioned Grendel as a cartoon figure in a cartoon world, and he establishes the arbitrary reality of this world on the first page, when Grendel says, "I let out a howl so unspeakable that the water at my feet turns sudden ice and even I myself am left uneasy."[4] This cartoon reality is further defined when, in a moment of frustration, Grendel smashes down some trees— and apologizes to those still standing: " 'No offense,' I say, with a terrible, sycophantish smile, and tip an imaginary hat" (7). And Grendel is still playing the cartoon clown at the end of the novel, when, moments before Beowulf rips his arm off, he bursts open the massive door to Hrothgar's meadhall with his fingertips and ties a tablecloth about his neck as if donning a bib for a feast—of thanes.

Gardner also creates a comic tension by having Grendel's narration combine contemporary American idiom and slang with the alliteration and figurative noun-compounds (or "kennings") of *Beowulf:* "Such are the tiresome memories of a shadow-shooter, earth-rim-roamer, walker of the world's weird wall" (7). But as his despair deepens, Grendel becomes a purer poet. He is less self-consciously alliterative and he registers his emotions and experiences in progressively more telling images—a shift in style which creates sympathy for his character, despite the ironic and distancing effect of Gardner's cartoon vision.

Gardner begins *Grendel* by immediately stepping outside *Beowulf* and saluting the opening lines of *The Canterbury Tales,* in which Chaucer alludes to April and the zodiac:

> Whan that Aprill with his shoures soote
> The droghte of March hath perced to the roote,
> . . . and the yonge sonne
> Hath in the Ram his halve cours yronne. . . . [5]

But Grendel's actions invert the tone and meaning of Chaucer's lines and give them the tenor of *The Waste Land,* in which "April is the cruellest month" because T. S. Eliot's characters are troubled by sexual feelings they wish to deny.[6] Grendel reacts similarly to the "old ram" standing before him. He yells at it, enraged at the surge of spring and sexuality that the creature exhibits—a connection with nature and feeling that Grendel rejects. To Chaucer's persona, the ram symbolizes Aries, the sun sign which marks the beginning of the

Understanding John Gardner

zodiacal year. But Grendel is unaware of the zodiac, and his naivete establishes an ironic perspective for the reader. To Grendel, the ram objectifies only his own "pointless" and "ridiculous" existence. All events, Grendel argues, echoing his nihilistic dragon, are "accidents," random and meaningless incidents of slippage in the "cold mechanics" (9) of the universe. To him, the "sun spins mindlessly overhead, the shadows lengthen and shorten as if by plan" (7). But he denies that there is a plan.

Gardner repeatedly indicated that Grendel's vision was inspired by Jean-Paul Sartre's *Being and Nothingness* (1943), which Gardner admired for its metaphors and style, but disliked for its ideas. Sartre's most famous metaphor is that of existential man peering into the abyss of nothingness and contemplating the suicide that will free him from his anguish: "I approach the precipice, and my scrutiny is searching for myself in my very depths. In terms of this moment, I play with my possibilities. My eyes, running over the abyss from top to bottom, imitate the possible fall and realize it symbolically. . . ."[7] Grendel echoes Sartre's existential "possibilities" and psychological "depths" when, one night, he looks down from a cliff over dark chasms and says, "once again I am aware of my potential: I could die. . . . I stand there shaking from head to foot, moved to the deep-sea depths of my being . . ." (10).

Since Grendel begins his narrative in the last year of his life, and the twelfth year of his war with Hrothgar, his character and vision have already been shaped by past events, which he records and narrates in extended flashbacks. In the process of the narrative, however, Grendel blurs the sequence of events, and some readers confuse cause and effect. Grendel did not, for example, become an existentialist when he discovered the "dragon"—an event recorded in chapter 5; rather, he became an existentialist when he was violently separated from his mother—an event recorded in chapter 2. Before he was separated from his mother, they were, he says in chapter 2, "one thing, like the wall and the rock growing out from it.— Or so [he] ardently, desperately affirmed" (17). But then he caught his foot between the joined trunks of two oaks, and when he "bellowed" (bull-like) for his mother, he attracted only a bull (Gardner's ironic salute to the sun sign Taurus). The bull, Grendel realized, fought "by instinct, blind mechanism ages old" (21), repeatedly goring the same place on his leg. From this experience, Grendel abstracted a vision of a mechanistic universe without spiritual connectedness, and he later attributes this vision to the dragon, who is inspired by the "solipsistic existentialism"[8] that Gardner identified with Sartre's philosophy. As Grendel says, bitterly, "I understood that the world was nothing: a mechanical chaos of casual, brute enmity on which we stupidly impose our hopes and fears. I understood that, finally and absolutely, I alone exist. All the rest, I saw, is merely what pushes me, or what I push against, blindly—as blindly as all that is not myself pushes back. I create the whole universe, blink by blink.—An ugly god pitifully dying in a tree!" (21–22). This perception, which parodies Sartre's passage on solipsism in *Being and Nothingness*,[9] leads Grendel to the nihilism that Gardner saw as the logical result of Sartre's emphasis on the self as the only consciousness that gives existence authentic meaning.

From this point forward in the narrative—told in flashback—Grendel is "an alien, the rock broken free of the wall" (23) that is his mother, his only spiritual connection. When he tries to communicate with Hrothgar and his thanes, they are terrified and Hrothgar hurls his ax—thus beginning what

Grendel refers to as their war. Disconnected spiritually from his inarticulate mother and unable to communicate with humanity, all Grendel can see is "meaningless objectness," "universal bruteness," and "pointless accident" (28); and he retreats into a parody of Sartrean self-consciousness: "I observe myself observing what I observe" (29).

Grendel is cynical about words, therefore, when he hears the Shaper pluck his harp, quote the opening lines of *Beowulf,* and make Hrothgar's meadhall (called "Hereot" or "Hart") ring with verses that reconstitute the past and glorify the present. Yet Grendel—like Mary Shelley's monster when he hears the blind man play the guitar—is profoundly touched by the blind Shaper when he plays the harp and recites his poetry. It creates, Grendel says, an emotional "fire more dread than any visible fire" (43). And overwhelmed by the contraries of faith and doubt, he departs (under Gemini: The Twins), a "ridiculous hairy creature torn apart by poetry—crawling, whimpering, streaming tears, across the world like a two-headed beast . . . and clutched the sides of my head as if to heal the split . . ." (44).

The Shaper offers a "vision without seams . . . the projected possible" (49). He speaks of the feud between Cain and Abel: how it divided the world between darkness and light; how Grendel was the "dark side," a member of the "terrible race God cursed" (51). And Grendel discovers that he wants the myth to be true, even though it makes him an "outcast, cursed by the rules of [the Shaper's] hideous fable" (55). But then he rejects the Shaper's fable, and, in a parody of Sartre's dictum that one should reject historical models and avoid "Bad Faith," he chooses a true self from within his consciousness. In doing so, he finds a dragon, a projection of his own despair and growing nihilism.

Though Gardner's critics generally discuss the dragon as if he were a character existing apart from Grendel's consciousness, he is in fact Grendel's own dark—or evil—self. Like Dorothy in *The Wizard of Oz,* who turns Kansas farmhands into the Cowardly Lion, the Strawman, and the Tinman, Grendel has an intensely realized fantasy or hallucination—in his case, of a dragon, a creation paralleled in *The Sunlight Dialogues* when Will Hodge Jr. sees Kleppmann as both an "elderly serpent" and the "Wizard of Oz."[10]

Gardner foreshadows Grendel's creation of the dragon by having him note how the artisans dip the sword blades in "snake's venom," and how one of the goldworkers seldom spoke, "except to laugh sometimes—'Nyeh heh heh' " (35). But then the darkness begins to hiss, snakelike, all around Grendel, like "some evil inside myself pushed out into the trees" (54); and, giving in to this projected evil, he makes his mind a blank and sinks "like a stone through earth and sea, toward the dragon" (56).

Synthesizing snake venom, gold, and the peculiar laugh of the goldworker, Grendel creates—or hallucinates—a dragon who sits on a mound of gold but almost falls off laughing ("Nyee he he he!") at the terrified Grendel, because he looks just "like a rabbit!" (59). Grendel has reason to be terrified by the evil he has projected: the dragon is a menacing as well as a fabulously grotesque creature who breathes fire and, in one of Gardner's many comic touches, warns Grendel not to sit directly in front of him in case he coughs. But this is the only concern for Grendel he shows. The dragon is the cold-eyed objectification of alienation, nihilism, and chaos—the incarnation of all that Grendel sees in his solipsistic existence after he is trapped in the oak trees and gives in to Sartrean existentialism.

The dragon ridicules the Shaper's vision of the universe. In doing so, Gardner has him cite (without attribution) whole passages from Whitehead's *Modes of Thought*—on "connectedness," "process," "types," "importance," the "essence of life," and the "bodily function of vegetables." But of these six topics only Whitehead's discussion of connectedness is crucial to an understanding of Gardner's central theme in the novel:

> A single fact in isolation is the primary myth required for finite thought, that is to say, for thought unable to embrace totality.
>
> This mythological character arises because there is no such fact. Connectedness is of the essence of all things of all types. It is of the essence of types, that they be connected. Abstraction from connectedness involves the omission of an essential factor in the fact considered. No fact is merely itself.[11]

In sneering at the limitations of the Shaper's vision, the dragon echoes Whitehead directly but out of context, suggesting that the Shaper and his audience have "no total vision, total system," and therefore they can only see "simple facts in isolation, and facts to connect them. . . . But there are no such facts. Connectedness is the essence of everything. . . . That's where the Shaper saves them. Provides an illusion of reality—puts together all their facts with a gluey whine of connectedness. Mere tripe, believe me. Mere sleight-of-wits. He knows no more than they do about total reality . . ." (64–65).

In characterizing the Shaper's vision of reality as a "gluey" mosaic of juxtaposed facts, rather than a total, organic whole, the dragon echoes Whitehead's argument that "connectedness is of the essence of all things of all types." But though the dragon quotes Whitehead's vision of reality almost verbatim, his sneering tone seems to undercut the validity of Whitehead's vision as well as the Shaper's. (Gardner is similarly ambiguous in chapter 9, where Grendel hears Ork, an ostensibly senile priest, quote Whitehead on "God.") Ultimately, the dragon sees the universe as all cogs, wheels, and accidents of evolution: "Things lock on, you know. The Devonian fish, the juxtaposed thumb, the fontanel, technology— *click click, click click* . . ." (71–72).

Though Gardner risks boring his readers, as well as Grendel, with the dragon's highly erudite and allusive monologue, the incongruity of a dragon lecturing a monster makes the chapter highly amusing and entertaining. Gardner's cartoon portrait of the dragon is richly imagined and humorous. Egocentric, miserly, nihilistic, and comically irascible, the dragon speaks of a meaningless and entropic universe, and his responses to Grendel's boredom are part of the humor: "It's damned hard, you understand, confining myself to concepts familiar to a creature of the Dark Ages" (67). But the dragon perseveres, and not only burdens Grendel with his vision of a meaningless universe, but offers him a glimpse of the future in a typically comic way: "A certain man will absurdly kill me. A terrible pity—loss of a remarkable form of life. Conservationists will howl" (70).

Rejecting historical models, Grendel looks, as Sartre requires, into his own consciousness and finds the "dragon," the incarnation of nihilism. Under the influence of this Sartrean dragon—the "evil inside" himself—Grendel projects himself as the "brute existent" by which humanity learns to define itself. He is a force, his dragon says, which drives humanity to "poetry, science, religion" (73).

Moreover, as in the epic, he is a force which is invulnerable to weapons. Unaware of Beowulf's lethal strength,

Grendel feels alienated from vulnerable humanity. Though initially happy with his new self, he realizes that his identity as a "brute existent" has still further isolated him from connectedness: "I was Grendel, Ruiner of Meadhalls, Wrecker of Kings! But also, as never before, I was alone" (80).

Unfairly matched against humanity, Grendel cannot be a hero, and he ridicules Unferth, refusing him a hero's death. Driven by despair and mounting nihilism, he almost kills the beautiful Wealtheow, whom he both idealizes and desires. And, ironically, though he defines himself as the personification of anarchy, he feels threatened when he hears the anarchistic dialogue of Hrothgar's young nephew Hrothulf and Hrothulf's mentor, "Red Horse" (Gardner's pun on the surname of the radical French philosopher Georges Sorel). Quoting and paraphrasing Sorel's *Reflections on Violence* (1908), Red Horse says that "the total ruin of institutions and morals is an act of creation. A *religious* act" (118), and that anarchy is the only solution, since "all systems are evil. All governments are evil. Not just a trifle evil. *Monstrously* evil" (120).

Striving, despite himself, for human connectedness, Grendel suddenly fears the loss of Hrothgar's political order, since his new identity as a "Wrecker of Kings" depends on kings to wreck. The dragon tells him that he drives humanity to "poetry, science, religion." But Grendel is himself driven to poetry, if not science and religion, when he realizes that physical destruction is finite. Anxious to punish Hrothgar, Grendel—in his developing role as a shaper—returns again to his traumatic experience in the oak trees. Quoting Thomas Kinsella's six-stanza poem "Wormwood," he gives Hrothgar a nightmare inspired by the moment when he threw his ax at Grendel and began their war. Of particular relevance are the last seven lines:

The two trunks in their infinitesimal dance of growth
Have turned completely about one another, their join
A slowly twisted scar . . . that I recognize. . . .

A quick arc flashes sidewise in the air,
A heavy blade in flight. A wooden stroke:
Iron sinks in the gasping core.
I will dream it again. (124)[12]

And so, by implication, will Grendel, since this poetic nightmare objectifies his loss of connectedness and his retreat into
solipsistic existentialism.

Gardner introduces metaphorical antitheses of mechanism vs. organicism throughout the novel, perhaps most notably when Grendel watches an archer (the symbol for the sun
sign Sagittarius) shoot a hart. Significantly, Grendel interprets
the archer's actions in the dragon's mechanistic terms: ". . .
the man's hand moves—click click click click—toward the
bow, and grasps it, and draws it down, away from the shoulder
and around in front (click click) . . ." (127). But when Grendel looks down at the newly dead hart, his vision is mystical
rather than mechanistic: "He lies as still as the snow hurtling
outward around him to the hushed world's rim. The image
clings to my mind like a growth. I sense some riddle in it"
(127). The answer to the riddle lies in the metaphor of spiritual
connectedness he once felt for his mother—when they were
"one thing, like the wall and the rock growing out from it." In
essence, the paradoxical life-in-death of the hart suggests that
the "click click" of mechanism is an illusion—that all life
(and death) is organic and connected.

Connectedness—with nature and with community—was
the only transcendence of the self that Gardner consistently affirmed in his fiction, and the reason that he was offended by
Sartre's metaphor of the alienated self. Though the image of

the archer was programmed by Gardner's commitment to his zodiacal structure, the paradox of the arrow's flight was inspired by Gardner's parody, once again, of *Being and Nothingness*. In his chapter on "Transcendence," Sartre cites—and dismisses as "naive"[13]—Zeno's paradoxical assertion that an arrow in flight is always at rest, since it is always where it is. Gardner ends his brief parody of Zeno/Sartre (previously parodied in *The Wreckage of Agathon*) by introducing a grotesque portrait of the aged and blind priest named Ork, who approaches, equally paradoxically, "like an arrow in a slowed-down universe . . ." (130).

Ork introduces allusions to Whitehead and inspires allusions to Blake. Grendel finds Ork awe-inspiring and vaguely threatening; and he defends himself against this feeling by pretending to be "The Destroyer"—the god Ork and the other priests pray to as Grendel's nemesis. When Grendel asks the blind Ork to tell him about "the King of the Gods," Ork echoes Whitehead, just as the dragon did. The dragon had mocked the Shaper's presentation of a connected universe by quoting Whitehead's *Modes of Thought* out of context. Ork, ostensibly senile, seems equally unreliable when he defines the idea of God using phrases from two of Whitehead's best-known works. Echoing *Science and the Modern World*, he says that God's "existence is the ultimate irrationality. . . . No reason can be given for the nature of God, because that nature is the ground of rationality" (131). Echoing *Process and Reality*, he concludes that God is the "*lure for our feeling* . . ." (132), whereas "the ultimate evil is that Time is perpetually perishing, and being actual involves elimination" (132). But finally, Gardner ties the Whiteheadian allusions more directly to the novel's central theme of connectedness: a young and seemingly fatuous priest tells Ork that he had feared for Ork's "bloodless rationalism," and launches into a rhapsodic sermon which emphasizes the transcendence of organicism and eternal connectedness while echoing Blake's anti-rationalism: ". . . merely rational thought leaves the mind incurably crippled in a closed and ossified system. . . . Both blood and sperm are explosive, irregular, feeling-pitched, messy—and inexplicably fascinating. They transcend. They leap the gap!" (135–36). Though Grendel dismisses the young priest's words as drunken ravings, they later echo in his mind as, caught in the agony of Beowulf's painful grip, he transcends his own alienating rationality, and Beowulf whispers— or seems to—that "the world will burn green, sperm build again" (170).

When the young priest says that Ork's "rational thought leaves the mind incurably crippled in a closed and ossified system," he is echoing the thematic resolution of Blake's fourth "Memorable Fancy" from *The Marriage of Heaven and Hell,* which Gardner quotes in fragments from the moment Grendel discovers the dragon in his consciousness. When Grendel first meets the dragon, he echoes Blake's vision of hell while seeming to fall through the dragon's giant eye into "a soundless void. . . . a black sun and spiders . . ." (61). Then when he meets Ork, Grendel associates Ork with the dragon and echoes Blake in greater detail: "A void boundless as a nether sky. I hang by the twisted roots of an oak, looking down into immensity. Vastly far away I see the sun, black but shining, and slowly revolving around it there are spiders" (137). Significantly, however, Gardner leaves out Blake's concluding vision of the Leviathan, a huge sea-dragon which personifies evil in Blake's vision of hell. As Blake sits in the "twisted root of an oak," he sees "the scaly fold of a monstrous serpent. . . . [I]t was the head of Leviathan. . . . & then this appearance was no more, but I found my sitting on a pleasant bank beside a river by moon light hearing a harper who sung to the harp, & his theme was, The man who never alters his opinion is like standing water, & breeds reptiles of the mind."[14] In leaving out Blake's vision of the dragon, the harper, and the anti-rationalistic conclusion, Gardner is trusting that a reader familiar with Blake's work will follow the analogy to its implicit conclusion, paralleling Grendel's dragon and Shaper with Blake's dragon and harper. But the theme of illusion is even more complex than Gardner's readers have suggested.[15] Grendel's "reptile of the mind" was, in Gardner's words, a "Sartrean dragon," the product of "Sartre's Existentialism," which Gardner equated with "perverse rationality"[16] and the medieval soul's corrupted "reason."[17]

Blake's poetry also inspired the name "Ork," Gardner's verbal echo of "Orc," the name of Blake's shape-shifting monster who appears in a cycle of poems including, Northrop Frye and Harold Bloom suggest, "The Mental Traveller,"[18] the source of Gardner's epigraph for *Grendel* and an important analogue. Orc's most significant associations in Blake's poetry are with the suffering of Prometheus (he is nailed down upon a rock) and the crucifixion of Christ. Essentially, Frye suggests, Orc is the "dying and reviving god of [Blake's] mythology."[19] As such, he takes many shapes and identities. He appears as the personification of political revolution, human imagination, and the "true poet"—all to a varying degree echoed by the character of Grendel, who becomes a true poet—or true "Shaper"—as the novel progresses. And though Orc is initially confined in a cave, his imagination is omniscient and he is ultimately associated, like Grendel, with a serpent, into which he shape-shifts after escaping his fetters. But Orc can also be Christ—though, as Bloom suggests, he "comes as a child of terror, Christ the Tyger rather than Christ the Lamb. . . ."[20]

In "The Mental Traveller," Orc undergoes a continuing metamorphosis, from birth to death to rebirth, beginning as a "Babe," who is tortured by an old woman and grows older as she grows younger. Gardner emphasizes this pattern of suffering and eternal recurrence by choosing the poem's third stanza for his epigraph:

> And if the Babe is born a Boy
> He's given to a Woman Old,
> Who nails him down upon a rock,
> Catches his shrieks in cups of gold.

Gardner systematically echoes this epigraph in chapter 2, at the point when Grendel is rescued as a babe from the oak trees by his mother, who has "a shriek ten times as loud" as Grendel's, "eyes as bright as dragonfire," and a smell which pours in "like blood into a silver cup . . ." (27–28). And again, as with the earlier allusions to this chapter, Gardner repeats the imagery at the end of the novel, reminding the reader of Grendel's Orcian identity when Beowulf rips off his arm: "I cry, I bawl like a baby. He stretches his blind white wings and breathes out fire" (172).

Gardner introduced both the Blakean allusions and the zodiacal structure relatively late in the novel's composition.[21] In adopting Blake's vision and imagery, he was attempting to reconcile the opposing ideas of connectedness (the Shaper/ Whitehead) and disconnectedness (the dragon/Sartre); and Orc's cycle of eternal recurrence in "The Mental Traveller" gave him a metaphor, though he bends it to his own use and ignores the poem's bleaker implications. At the same time Gardner was trying to solve the even more fundamental problem of organizing some short tales about Grendel into a novel, and the zodiac gave him a structure.

Though Grendel describes various incarnations of the zodiac's twelve sun signs throughout the novel, this is the reader's ironic perception, since Grendel does not know the zodiac exists and he denies there is any meaning to the motion of the stars.[22] Indeed, the textual evidence suggests that Gardner periodically abandoned his original intention of showing the astrological influence of the sun signs on Grendel. Consequently, Gardner later confused students of the novel when he suggested to Joe David Bellamy that the novel's major ideas were attached to the zodiac: "In *Grendel* I wanted to go through the main ideas of Western civilization—which seemed to me about . . . twelve?" When Bellamy asked if he developed all twelve ideas, Gardner responded, "It's got twelve chapters. They're all hooked to astrological signs, for instance, and that gives you nice easy clues."[23] But critics have found the "clues" less than easy. Susan Strehle suggests that a list would include "imperialism, mysticism, materialism, solipsism, and anarchism."[24] And a list might also include organicism, mechanism, idealism, nihilism, heroism, and love. But Gardner was not as methodical in exploring ideas in the novel as he implied to Bellamy—or to Gregory Morris, who was told that the chapters correspond to the "twelve Aristotelian virtues."[25] This led Morris to Aristotle's *Nichomachean Ethics*—and the conclusion that Aristotle's prescribed virtues were not particularly relevant to *Grendel*. Finally, as David Cowart observes,

> the important ideas explored in the book number rather more than twelve: Gardner manages to scan major social and economic ideas like chivalry, feudalism, and mercantilism; theology from primitive animism to Kierkegaard, with side glances at oriental reli-

gions; metaphysics from Hume to Sartre and from Heidegger to Whitehead; and political philosophy—the origins, legitimacy, and accountability of the state—from Plato to Locke and Hobbes, and from Machiavelli to Marx and Georges Sorel.[26]

In short, Gardner's later comments about his intentions in *Grendel* are better thought of as creative reactions to the process, rather than re-creations of the process. Though the zodiac gave Gardner a structural principle, his philosophical allusions and ideas are only periodically—and then arbitrarily—related to the sun signs. For example: though his introduction of a living ram (for Aries) is clearly appropriate as the incarnation of spring and new life, his introduction of a living bull under Taurus (the Bull) as a symbol of mechanism is arbitrary and ironic. And while his portrayal of Grendel's spiritually divided self under Gemini (the Twins) and the Shaper's vision under the mystical water sign Cancer (the Crab) are appropriate, his association of the nihilistic dragon with Leo (the Lion)—traditionally linked with the sun, gold, and God—will strike most students of astrology as an ironic inversion, as will the location of Unferth's quest for heroism under Virgo: the harvest Virgin. (In this case, Gardner actually forces the association by having Grendel pelt apples at Unferth until "he was crying, only a boy, famous hero or not: a poor miserable virgin.") On the other hand, Gardner's portrayal of Wealtheow under Libra (the Scales) seems quite fitting, since she is composed, courteous, and altruistic. She creates a political balance when she marries Hrothgar, and—temporarily—an emotional balance between the divided selves of Grendel, who, captivated by her queenliness and beauty, decides that to kill her would be the ultimate act of nihilism. But though the political scheming of Red Horse and Hrothulf is appropriate under Scorpio (the Scorpion),

Gardner's focus on the mechanism and mysticism of the arrow's flight in relation to Sagittarius (the Archer) is quite arbitrary, though obviously important to the theme of connectedness.

As noted, Gardner argued that Sartre's existentialism led to a "perverse rationality," which in turn led to nihilism and thence to greater perversity and despair. To objectify the monstrous perversity of Grendel's nihilism, Gardner associates it, again arbitrarily, with an incarnation of Capricorn (the Goat) which climbs mechanically toward Grendel, while he continues to hurl objects at it even after he knows the creature's brain is dead. Grendel's actions reflect the despair he feels over the approaching death of the Shaper, but Gardner distances the reader emotionally by having Grendel say "So it goes" (142), echoing Kurt Vonnegut's phrase and death motif in *Slaughterhouse-Five,* which Gardner later criticized in *On Moral Fiction* for its "seeming cold-heartedness."[27]

Gardner suggested in interviews that his major problem with the novel was keeping Grendel alive, once Beowulf had arrived at Hrothgar's court. In postponing the inevitable moment, however, Gardner builds suspense and anticipation, repeatedly foreshadowing Beowulf's arrival and emphasizing Grendel's excitement over Beowulf's incredible strength and brutal courage. Known only as the "stranger" to Grendel, Beowulf seems "mechanical" and "machine"-like. The ultimate paradox of the novel is, however, that his cold-blooded brutality generates Grendel's spiritual connectedness, and Gardner ironically echoes the traditional symbolism of Beowulf as a Christ figure. Grendel's mother warns him to "*beware the fish*" (149), and, shortly after, he sees that Beowulf has "no more beard than a fish" (154), and that his shoulders are as "sleek as the belly of a shark . . ." (155).

And finally, though he remains unaware of the zodiac, Grendel dies under the sign of the Fish.

Grendel more consciously and confusedly associates Beowulf with the dragon. As Grendel says, "I have seen—I embody—the vision of the dragon . . ." (158). He foreshadows his vision of Beowulf as a dragon when he says "I could drop into a trance just looking at those shoulders" (155), and he almost does so, saying "I found something peculiar happening to my mind. His mouth did not seem to move with his words, and the harder I stared at his gleaming shoulders, the more uncertain I was of their shape" (163–64). Then he smells the "scent" of the dragon, and remembers "twisted roots, an abyss . . ." (164)—imagery associated with Blake's vision of hell.

Grendel first discovered the dragon when he went into an Oz-like trance and projected his evil self. Now, when Beowulf clasps Grendel's hand, it has, Grendel thinks, the crushing force of a "dragon's jaws" (168). But still desperately playing the clown, Grendel describes himself as "grotesquely shaking hands" with his "long-lost brother . . ." (168–69). Significantly, this fatal handshake brings him "suddenly awake. The long pale dream, [his] history, falls away" (169), and he moves toward spiritual connectedness, momentarily free of illusion, thus momentarily free of the abstraction that separates him from a perception of existence and/or reality. When he feels pain again, however, he sees "fiery wings" coming from Beowulf's shoulders, and he jerks his "head, trying to drive out illusion. The world is what it is and always was. That's our hope, our chance. Yet even in times of catastrophe we people it with tricks. Grendel, Grendel, hold fast to what is true!" (169).

But Grendel finds it profoundly difficult. In his agony, he is more and more the victim of illusion—of abstraction—and readers are sometimes misled by their growing empathy with his character,[28] as was Gardner, who said that he wrote the ending in a "trancelike state,"[29] a creative process which may account for his contradictory statements of intention to various interviewers. Crucial to understanding what is true (and what is illusion) is the knowledge that Beowulf exists outside Grendel's mind, but that the dragon does not. Crucial also is Grendel's previous dissociation of Beowulf from his speech. Having repeatedly observed that Beowulf's mouth does not "seem to move with his words," Grendel hears (or imagines that he hears) Beowulf whisper and seemingly mock the words of the dragon, beginning with "*A meaningless swirl in the stream of time . . .*" (170). But if Grendel projected the original dragon on the world outside his mind, then, given his dissociative response to Beowulf's speech, he is apparently projecting meaning and words on Beowulf's whispering, along with the flames in Beowulf's mouth, and the wings in Beowulf's shoulders. There are ambiguous moments, however, where Beowulf seems to generate his dialogue outside of Grendel's consciousness.

Gardner interpreted the original Beowulf of the epic as a Christ figure, and uses the widely recognized symbol of the fish to identify Beowulf with Christ in the novel. But the association of dragon imagery with Christ has less currency for most readers, and Gardner acknowledged the problem of interpretation when he explained that he had in mind the two dragons of medieval art: "There's Christ the dragon, and there's Satan the dragon. There's always a war between these two great dragons. In modern Christian symbolism a sweeter image of Jesus with the sheep in his arms has evolved, but I like the old image of the warring dragon."[30] The novel, however, does not stress this thematic antithesis in clearly opposing images. Instead, Gardner repeatedly echoes Blake, who identified Orc as a ''serpent,'' sometimes alluding to Satan, sometimes to Christ, and sometimes dramatizing the thematic oppositions—or ''contraries''—of good and evil in the same Orcian figure—as in *The Four Zoas,* where, as Bloom suggests, Orc becomes ''Christ the Tyger.'' In short, though Gardner's epigraph introduces the Orcian monster of ''The Mental Traveller,'' he synthesizes this vision of the monster with allusions to Orc from Blake's other works.

Gardner later observed that Beowulf ''says everything that William Blake would say. Blake says a wonderful thing: 'I look upon the dark satanic mills; I shake my head; they vanish.' That's it. That's right. You *redeem* the world by acts of imagination. . . .''[31] Grendel's acts of imagination are, however, corrupting rather than redemptive until he experiences the physical agony that leads to his death. Only then does he give up the irony and cynicism that once inspired his parody of Anglo-Saxon poetry (''these brainless budding trees, these brattling birds'' [6]) and that led him to imagine a nihilistic dragon and to mock the idea of connectedness that the Shaper had affirmed. But now Grendel, humanized by despair and grief over the Shaper's death, ''becomes the Shaper,''[32] as Gardner later observed, and moves toward redemption.

A dominant pattern in these last pages of the novel is Grendel's gradual return to a paradoxical state of innocence beyond illusion. Trying to shut out Beowulf's words—imagined or real—Grendel cries out ''Mama!'' (170) and moves, in his agony, toward a symbolic infancy in parallel to Blake's ''Babe'' in ''The Mental Traveller.'' When Grendel was trapped in the oak trees, he decided that he was in his mother's eyes ''an alien, the rock broken free of the wall.'' After she saved him, he tried unsuccessfully to ''smash through the

walls of her unconsciousness'' (28) and regain the feeling
of connectedness. Gardner develops this metaphor of connectedness when Beowulf symbolically smashes the walls of
Grendel's consciousness—and unconsciousness—by cracking
his head against the meadhall. As this happens, Grendel imagines—or hears—Beowulf speaking of a Blakean faith in the
power of the imagination to create either a hell or a heaven of
experience: *"You make the world by whispers, second by second. Are you blind to that? Whether you make it a grave or a
garden of roses is not the point. Feel the wall: is it not hard?*
(171) Then Beowulf smashes Grendel's head again, and forces
him to sing of ''walls.''

After a false start, Grendel does sing of walls, closely
echoing the last stanza of Gardner's poem ''Setting for an Old
Welsh Line'':

> The wall will fall to the wind as the windy hill
> will fall, and all things thought in former times:
> Nothing made remains, nor man remembers.
> And these towns shall be called the shining towns! (172)

Grendel has not only learned that all things fade, he has, as a
Shaper, gained control over his imagination. A year earlier he
acknowledged that he had spent his whole life ''spinning a
web of words, pale walls of dreams, between myself and all I
see'' (8). But now, caught in Beowulf's lethal grasp, he creates a poem. He is momentarily able to pierce the ''pale walls
of dreams'' that turn into Blakean nightmares; able, that is,
to focus on existential events and reject the distorting abstractions that keep him from the connectedness affirmed by
the Shaper (and Whitehead), but mocked by the dragon
(and Sartre).

When Beowulf rips off his arm, Grendel travels still further toward innocence: he cries ''like a baby'' and, in his ag-

ony, it seems to him that Beowulf "stretches his blinding white wings and breathes out fire" (172). Fighting against this illusion, Grendel flees into the night, leaving Beowulf behind, but seeing flames and winged men everywhere—until he tells himself "*Think!*" and comes "suddenly awake once more from the nightmare" and sees the "cold-blooded objectness" of existence (172).

Grendel cries out to his mother that he is dying; that Beowulf's victory was an "accident," and that the world is still "blind, mindless, mechanical" (173). But he again gives into illusion and comes to what he calls a "nightmare cliff." At the beginning of the novel, Gardner parodies Sartre's metaphor of the existential cliff by describing Grendel at the edge of a real cliff, screaming "dark chasms! . . . seize me!" and "shaking from head to foot, moved to the deep-sea depths of [his] being . . . (10). He has now in fact returned to that cliff. Despite Beowulf's reality instruction, however, Grendel is still spinning "walls of dreams," and still under the influence of the Sartrean dragon. Consequently, he can only—for the moment—see the "nightmare" cliff overlooking Blake's vision of hell, which Grendel hallucinated when he first discovered the dragon and which he now hallucinates again: "I cling to the huge twisted roots of an oak. I look down past stars to a terrifying darkness" (173). Though he seems to recognize the place, he knows that it is "impossible" because it is the setting for his nightmare vision of the dragon. Yet still in the nightmare, he responds to the dragon and, though already bleeding to death, he feels a compulsion to hasten his death by committing suicide: "Standing baffled, quaking with fear, three feet from the edge of a nightmare cliff, I find myself incredibly moving toward it. I look down, down, into bottomless blackness, feeling the dark power moving in me like an ocean current, some monster inside me, deep sea wonder, dread night monarch astir in his cave, moving me slowly to my voluntary tumble into death'' (173). But Grendel resists the nihilistic reptile of his mind, his Sartrean dragon (''deep sea wonder, dread night monarch astir in his cave''),[33] and he does not commit suicide.

Contrary to some readings of the text, Grendel neither jumps nor imagines he jumps. Instead, as Gardner emphasizes, the ''nightmare cliff'' disappears: ''Again sight clears. I discover I no longer feel pain'' (173). And significantly, when the pain ends, the illusions end: he sees not the ''nightmare cliff'' overlooking the Blakean abyss of hell, but the ''existential'' cliff overlooking the dark chasms at which he had screamed (''seize me'') one year earlier. He has come full circle. As he looks at his body, ''slick with blood,'' he does indeed feel the existential anguish that Sartre describes—but he does not jump. Instead, he affirms life. In the words Gardner used to describe the antagonists of *The Sunlight Dialogues,* Grendel is driven to ''a bedrock humanness, stripped of illusion, full of grace.'' Free of the distorting abstractions of words—free of all illusions—he returns to a childlike innocence and the world as it is. But like Orc, he is still a monster, and he feels rage against those who sought to destroy him, even though, paradoxically, he feels the joy of spiritual connectedness. Unable to separate joy from rage, however, he looks at the gathered animals who have come to watch him die, and he ends his narrative, first with a question, then with a curse—which turns out to be a blessing:

> *Is it joy I feel?*
> They watch on, evil, incredibly stupid, enjoying my destruction.

"Poor Grendel's had an accident," I whisper. "*So may you all.*"

Gardner—asked to interpret Grendel's final words—responded, "when the first Shaper dies, a kid is chosen to succeed him, but the real successor is Grendel. In the last pages of the book Grendel begins to apprehend the whole universe: life and death, his own death. Poetry is an accident, the novel says, but it's a great one. May it happen to all of us."[34] But readers still detected the tone of a curse in Grendel's parting words, and Gardner later attempted to explain the paradox: "That's of course the old Presbyterian in me . . . the grace doctrine; that is to say, you don't win by your own efforts, and in the world that I understand; that is to say, this world we are in, this terminal world, finally love happens to you. . . . Everything happens to Grendel. Grendel resisted desperately from beginning to end but when he says, 'Poor Grendel has had an accident. So may you all,' it seems to me that's a blessing as well as a curse."[35]

In offering up this unconscious—or involuntary—blessing, Grendel joins Fred Clumly and other Gardner protagonists who echo Coleridge's vision of accidental grace in *The Rime of the Ancient Mariner*—a moment which Gardner also associated with the vision of William Blake."[36] Though Grendel starts out to curse his enemies, he feels the "*joy*" of connectedness and, as Gardner suggests, the poetic intuition that his "accident" is benevolent and meaningful. Thus, his curse turns into a blessing, though—like the Ancient Mariner—he is unaware that it is a blessing when he utters it.

Grendel followed the spirit of Sartre's directive: instead of emulating an ethical model of behavior, he looked into his own consciousness—and found a nihilistic dragon. This dragon, echoing Blake's vision in *The Marriage of Heaven and Hell*, became a "reptile of the mind." When Blake's vision of the evil dragon ends, he finds himself on the bank of the river, listening to a harper. But Grendel's harper—or "Shaper"—is dead. Instead, Grendel has become his own Shaper, and when he shakes his head against the illusion of the dragon he sees an unmediated reality, and returns to a paradoxical innocence born of the contraries of faith and doubt. Feeling at one with the universe, including his "brother" Beowulf, Grendel asks himself in wonderment, "*Is it joy I feel?*" In doing so, he discovers the only spiritual redemption that Gardner, like Blake, consistently affirmed.[37]

NOTES

1. John Gardner, *The Construction of Christian Poetry in Old English* (Carbondale: Southern Illinois University Press, 1975) 83–84.

2. See John Gardner, *The Art of Fiction: Notes on Craft for Young Writers* (New York: Knopf, 1984) 185.

3. For a facsimile of Gardner's notes on *Grendel*, see John M. Howell, *John Gardner: A Bibliographical Profile* (Carbondale: Southern Illinois University Press, 1980) 115.

4. John Gardner, *Grendel* (New York: Knopf, 1971) 5. Parenthetical page references in the text are to this edition.

5. Geoffrey Chaucer, *The Works of Geoffrey Chaucer,* ed. F. N. Robinson, 2nd ed. (Boston: Houghton Mifflin, 1957) 17.

6. See David Cowart, *Arches & Light: The Fiction of John Gardner* (Carbondale: Southern Illinois University Press, 1983) 46.

7. Jean-Paul Sartre, *Being and Nothingness,* trans. Hazel E. Barnes (New York: Philosophical Library, 1956) 32.

8. John Gardner, interview with author, Susquehanna, Pa., 6 August 1980. By permission of the Estate of John Gardner and Georges Borchardt, Inc.

9. Sartre 229–32.

10. John Gardner, *The Sunlight Dialogues* (New York: Knopf, 1972) 571.

11. Alfred North Whitehead, *Modes of Thought* (1938; New York: Free-Press Macmillan, 1968) 9.

12. Gardner changes Kinsella's punctuation and spacing; see Thomas Kinsella, "Wormwood," *Poems 1956–1973* (Winston-Salem, N.C.: Wake Forest University Press, 1979) 68.

Notes

13. Sartre 210.
14. *The Poetry and Prose of William Blake,* ed. David V. Erdman, rev. ed. (Garden City, N.Y.: Doubleday, 1970) 40–41.
15. See Cowart 207 n. 12; Michael Ackland, "Blakean Sources in John Gardner's *Grendel,*" *Critique* 23 (1981): 57–66; and Helen B. Ellis and Warren Ober, "*Grendel* and Blake: The Contraries of Existence," *John Gardner: Critical Perspectives,* ed. Robert A. Morace and Kathryn VanSpanckeren (Carbondale: Southern Illinois University Press, 1982) 46–61.
16. Ed Christian, "An Interview with John Gardner," *Prairie Schooner* 54 (Winter 1981): 81.
17. As Gregory L. Morris points out, Gardner has in mind the tripartite soul of medieval psychology: the *rational,* the *irascible,* and the *concupiscent;* see Morris, *A World of Order and Light: The Fiction of John Gardner* (Athens: University of Georgia Press, 1984) 52–56.
18. Gardner's interpretation of Orc's significance in "The Mental Traveller" was largely influenced by Northrop Frye, *Fearful Symmetry* (Princeton: Princeton University Press, 1947) 227–29; and Harold Bloom, *Blake's Apocalypse* (Garden City, N.Y.: Doubleday, 1963) 289–97.
19. Frye 207.
20. Bloom 297.
21. John Gardner, interview with author.
22. For detailed studies of the astrological signs in *Grendel,* see David Minugh, "John Gardner Constructs *Grendel*'s Universe," *Studies in English Philology, Linguistics, and Literature,* ed. Mats Ryden and Lennart A. Bjork (Stockholm: Almquist & Wiksell, 1978) 125–41; Craig J. Stromme, "The Twelve Chapters of *Grendel,*" *Critique* 20 (1978): 83–92; and Barry Fawcett and Elizabeth Jones, "The Twelve Traps in John Gardner's *Grendel,*" *American Literature* 62 (Dec. 1990): 634–35.
23. Joe David Bellamy and Pat Ensworth, "John Gardner," *The New Fiction: Interviews with Innovative American Writers,* ed. Joe David Bellamy (Urbana: University of Illinois Press, 1974) 173–74.
24. Susan Strehle, "John Gardner's Novels: Affirmation and the Alien," *Critique* 18 (1976): 94.
25. Morris 235–36 n. 12.
26. Cowart 43.
27. John Gardner, *On Moral Fiction* (New York: Basic Books, 1978) 87.
28. The reader's empathy with Grendel's character leads to contradictory interpretations; see Robert Merrill, "John Gardner's *Grendel* and the Interpretation of Modern Fables," *American Literature* 56 (May 1984): 162–80.
29. John Gardner, *On Becoming a Novelist* (New York and London: Harper & Row, 1983) 57–61.
30. Paul F. Ferguson, John R. Maier, Frank McConnell, and Sara Matthiessen. "The Art of Fiction LXXIII: John Gardner," *Paris Review* 21

(Spring 1979): 44–45. Rpt. in *Writers at Work, Sixth Series,* ed. George Plimpton (New York: Viking, 1984).

31. Bellamy and Ensworth 178.

32. Bellamy and Ensworth 179.

33. Twelve years later, in *On Becoming a Novelist* (1983), Gardner ignores the dragon and contradicts his contemporaneous interpretation, suggesting that, in ''willing his death, Grendel is unconsciously trying to please God so that God will not slaughter him,'' but that in willing his own death, Grendel is, at the same time, ''defying the God he hates and fears'' (60).

34. Bellamy and Ensworth 180.

35. ''John Gardner: A Defense Against Darkness,'' *The Originals: The Writer in America* (PBS, 3 April 1978).

36. John Gardner, interview with author.

37. For a discussion of Blake's idea of redemption, see Alfred Kazin, ''Introduction,'' *The Portable Blake,* ed. Alfred Kazin (1946; New York: Viking Press, 1968): 25.

CHAPTER FIVE

The King's Indian:
Stories and Tales

Herbert Fink won the Society of Illustrators' Gold Medal Award for his illustrations of *The King's Indian* (1974), one of Gardner's most attractive as well as technically innovative books. The stories and tales, including the novella "The King's Indian," were written between spring 1971 and spring 1974, and some were published in magazines before Gardner collected them. They offer a wide range of formal experimentation and perspective. As Gardner told Marshall Harvey, "everything in *The King's Indian* is about literary form and literary form as a vehicle of vision. . . . The true story teller, like Jonathan Upchurch, in "The King's Indian," is a model for all artists—intuition in the service of King Reason—therefore the eternal artist, God on earth."[1]

Gardner had experimented with the romance and the epic in *The Sunlight Dialogues, Grendel,* and *Jason and Medeia.* In *The King's Indian* he explores shorter forms. Dominating the collection is the form of the "tale," which Gardner preferred over the "story" because it did not require a fine-grained illusion of reality. As he points out in his textbook *The Forms of Fiction,* the author of a tale maintains the illusion of truth by avoiding "comparison with the world of the actual."[2] Though Gardner sometimes breaks this rule to achieve comic incongruities, especially with his use of anachronisms, he generally follows the Gothic tradition of locating his tale in a remote time and place while emphasizing details that have their own reality. Similarly, though the characters in his tales may possess superhuman or unnatural powers, he maintains their fictive reality by avoiding comparisons to ordinary people and everyday problems, and by giving them an emotional truth that allows the reader to accept them as real despite their unreal context.

Gardner divides *The King's Indian* into three "Books." As a transition from the real world to the surreal world of his tales, he begins "Book One: The Midnight Reader" with a realistic story, "Pastoral Care," then moves into the Gothic and the fabulous with "The Ravages of Spring," "The Temptation of St. Ivo," and "The Warden." He ends this section with the autobiographical story "John Napper Sailing Through the Universe," a tentatively realistic narrative which threatens to move into the surreal at any moment, thus offering a transition to "Book Two: Tales of Queen Louisa," whose mad heroine lives in the completely surreal world of "Queen Louisa," "King Gregor and the Fool," and "Muriel." Finally, in the third "Book," Gardner ends with one of his most ambitious metafictions: "The King's Indian: A Tale."

"Pastoral Care"

"Pastoral Care," a realistic story about moral anarchy, is set in Carbondale, Illinois, the home of Southern Illinois University, where Gardner taught at the time of the story (c. 1970)—during the height of the often violent demonstrations against the Vietnam War. Gardner, who sometimes described himself as a religious—though skeptical—conservative, explores personal concerns through the protag-

onist and narrator, Eugene Pick, the liberal minister of
Carbondale's Presbyterian church. Pick wears a beard—a
symbol of political radicalism at this time—and he delights in
shocking the conservative members of his church. He cannot
help feeling superior to those who come to him for spiritual
consolation. What could he have told Miss Ellis, a piano
teacher looking for "metronomic" certainty after her mother
died and life seemed "meaningless"? "I could have told
her—I hinted at it—that that was the point of Christianity. All
systems fail: psychologies, sociologies, philosophies, ritu-
als. . . . We follow not a system but a man, I could have said.
A conviction, a vital spirit."[3] And when John Grewy, M.D.,
says that his soul is "in torment," Pick retreats into abstraction, comparing himself to troubled poets who search for truth,
and asking, "Who'd need salvation if life were art?" (13).

To win salvation—or Gardner's earthbound version of
it—Pick must, like James Chandler, suppress his isolating
pride and affirm his faith in humanity and community. But his
arrogance isolates him from his flock. After a bearded Vietnam veteran—rumored to have blown up the University Art
Department (Gardner's fiction)—tells Pick that his sermon
"blew" his mind (Gardner's irony), Pick is inspired to even
more violent rhetoric. He delivers an inflammatory sermon on
how the parable of Christ's cursing the barren fig tree is a criticism of "dead, sham religion" (27), failing to recognize the
personal implications, and declaring that if "Caesar usurps
the rule of God, . . . blow up the Pentagon" (28).

After the anarchistic veteran blows up the Carbondale
police station, Reverend Pick flees eastward on a train. He
knows that Dr. Grewy would forgive his spiritual weakness.
But Dr. McGiver, a fellow passenger on the train, is, by
contrast and in counterpoint, interested only in his body.

When McGiver makes a sexual overture, Pick reaches an ironic—if homophobic—epiphany: "*Fruit,* I think, and am back to the fig tree, to fruitless Pick. And if my life is fruitless, does it matter?" (32).

Gardner, of course, believes it does, and moments after Pick has looked into his own barren soul, the train shudders to a halt, and he is outside with Dr. McGiver, trying to shield himself from the vision of a "stoned" and pregnant "hippie" woman, who has fallen from the train and is dying, yet with her "enormous pregnant abdomen in labor, a face smashed featureless, dripping hair, the dead stock of a tree. 'Christ,' the doctor whispers" (33). Responding to this elaborately symbolic scene, Pick undergoes a spiritual resurrection. He reaches out to the woman's half-crazed lover, and in his first unconscious gesture of some years, he transcends pride and spiritual isolation: "I am no one, for the moment; a disembodied voice; God's minister" (34). He pierces the walls of intellect and finds the truth of feeling: " 'Trust me,' I say. (The fall is endless. All systems fail.) I force myself to continue. I have no choice." Like earlier characters in Gardner's fiction, Pick finds grace through a gesture of compassion. By giving himself up to an act of faith, by blessing the man before him, he finds spiritual redemption.

"The Ravages of Spring"

Gardner read Edgar Allan Poe's Gothic tales with both affection and amusement. "The Ravages of Spring" is one of three stories in *The King's Indian,* including the title novella, which parodies Poe's work. Gardner's first-person narrator, a country doctor, apologizes for lacking Poe's poetic soul because the tale he is about to tell deserves Poe's talents. Nevertheless, he promises to do the best he can, and he suggests that it is a good thing that he is a rationalist, rather than a "Platonist" like Mr. Poe, for only a rationalist could be trusted with reporting his bizarre tale.

The modest doctor is fifty-four years old, and he is living in southern Illinois in the late nineteenth century. He writes that "we always have tornadoes in the spring, down in southern Illinois" (36). But the violent winds which initiate the story and stimulate the doctor's mad gallop with his horse (named "Shakespeare") are identified as "three enormous black cyclones . . ." (40), a word foreign to southern Illinois usage but crucial to Gardner's pun on the word "clone."

When the three cyclones spook Shakespeare, he takes his own head and gallops to a Gothic house with a high tower near a graveyard, where the doctor meets a red-haired man with buck teeth and enormous, gazellelike eyes, who introduces himself as "Professor John Hunter." Recognizing the name of an infamous and long-dead geneticist the doctor decides "Hunter" is mad and that he should therefore disguise his true identity by calling himself "Dr. William Thorpe." When a young woman enters, the doctor is struck by her appearance, which Gardner characterizes in a parody of Poe's style and imagery: "Her hair was black, perhaps Italian, possibly Semitic, but some sickness (I suspected a cancer of the blood) had robbed her of the bloom one expects in Mediterraneans and had left her face moonlike, lusterless. She was twenty or twenty-five, not older. Her eyes, limpid brown, were startling if you happened to compare them with her husband's . . ." (49). But the resemblance to her "husband" is more than coincidental, as Hunter soon explains, thrusting a daguerreotype of the original—and elderly—Professor John Hunter into the doctor's hand: " 'That man is my father. Or, rather, that man is my identical self. And this woman—' He swung to point at her. 'This woman is my mother, my wife, my sister. We're not *human*, Dr. Thorpe. We're *copies!—klones!*' " (55) Moreover, Gardner hints, they have somehow been produced by cyclones. And when four more cyclones now appear, like the "Bible's Four Horsemen" (57), Hunter, "mad as Faust—nay mad as Lucifer" (55), forces his mother-wife-sister and Dr. Thorpe up the tower steps toward an "ungodly" laboratory reminiscent of *Frankenstein*. But not listening to the "voice of the cyclone, or of God" (57), Thorpe dives down the stairs and escapes death with Hunter and his polymorphous companion.

When the doctor regains consciousness, however, he looks into the storm cellar and discovers "three small, wet, bawling children—boys. . . . red-headed, buck-toothed, and pale as ghosts" (59). They are, Thorpe later realizes, clones of "John Hunter cruelly resurrected" (65)—and apparently by the cyclones that destroyed him, though the situation is ambiguous. And despite Dr. Hunter's claim that he and the other clones are "not *human*" (55), Dr. Thorpe discovers (in a thematic contradiction that Gardner does not resolve) that the "souls of those three lost children . . . were unquiet . . . but I had no medicine for the human soul . . ." (60–65); nevertheless, he is forced to take personal charge of their well-being after a hired nurse accidentally drowns one of them while trying to purify its spirit.

Jeff Henderson observes that, in addition to Poe, Gardner parodies Kafka's story "A Country Doctor," which is echoed by Gardner's country doctor, who "is baffled but tries to behave rationally in an irrational situation,"[4] and has, like Kafka, a strangely behaving horse. It is questionable, however, whether the Kafkaesque analogue sufficiently detaches the reader from the sympathy generated by the God-abandoned, yet "human," infants.

"The Temptation of St. Ivo"

"The Temptation of St. Ivo" is perhaps more successful than "The Ravages of Spring" because Gardner is more engaged with its central character and theme. Like so many of his fictions, the story focuses on the battles between faith and nihilism, order and disorder, art and life. Brother Ivo, a rotund little monk of fifty, has spent his adult life illuminating manuscripts in a medieval monastery. Though recognized for his surpassing skill, and holding to his belief that he is doing God's work, he has remained spiritually inhibited in his art as well as his life, since both are dependent on following the strict rules of his religious order.

These rules forbid a monk either to talk or to leave the monastery. But Brother Ivo is tempted to break both rules by Brother Nicholas, who, unlike Brother Ivo, is tall, muscular, and desultory in his art. In a conflict echoing Robert Browning's "The Soliloquy of the Spanish Cloister,"[5] Brother Nicholas—the incarnation of chaos, a satanic figure—whispers to Brother Ivo, trying to provoke him into talking while they illuminate manuscripts and the other monks pretend not to hear. Brother Ivo fears he will break his vows of silence, and he echoes the philosopher Boethius: "The World is a river, and he who resists the pressure of Time and Space will be overwhelmed by it" (70). To escape further temptation, he has himself transferred to the fields, but Brother Nicholas follows, whispering that cosmic order is illusory.

Brother Ivo ultimately defines a new self and vision in response to his metaphysical threat, moving toward a spiritual freedom beyond the rules of his religious order and, implicitly, the restrictive conventions of allegory which limit his art. Though he does not believe in mythological creatures, he believes in the truths they symbolize, and his greatest achievement is a skillful drawing and illumination of the mythical Phoenix.

Brother Nicholas praises Brother Ivo's artistic achievement, but Brother Ivo senses his indifference to the art as well as its promise of resurrection out of self-immolating fire. Indeed, Brother Nicholas is inspired to evil, rather than good, by the painting: he tells Brother Ivo that he has discovered the whereabouts of the Phoenix and plans to leave the monastery and kill it. Though Brother Ivo is skeptical, his confessor suggests that the "Phoenix" may in fact be Brother Nicholas's symbol for an innocent child, or man's immortal soul, or the Virgin Mary; or perhaps his cry for help in facing what he sees as a God-abandoned universe. In fact, the confessor suggests, if Brother Ivo broke the rules and left the monastery to save the Phoenix, it "would be the act of a saint, a soul whose purity is beyond the rules that protect and keep the rest of us" (82).

Though this argument invites prideful sin, and though Brother Ivo discovers that the so-called confessor is really Brother Nicholas, he nevertheless follows Brother Nicholas into the forest, determined to save the Phoenix, whatever it may symbolize. But in doing so, he becomes Brother Nicholas's victim—the "Phoenix" he is trying to save. In his painting of the Phoenix, Brother Ivo had created an "interlace so complex as to baffle the mind as God's providence baffles, his mysterious workings, secret order in the seemingly pathless

universal forest'' (77). Outside the monastery Brother Ivo discovers an existential counterpoint to his painting: the trees
grow with ''interlocked beams like a roof above,'' and he is
''afraid, sick unto death with fear'' (87). He can find no path,
no order, and he temporarily loses faith in the goodness of
the universe.

When he meets a knight in the dark and pathless forest,
he imagines there is no one inside the armor, and he realizes
that the ''rules, techniques of a lifetime devoted to allegory
have ruined [him]'' (88). But after the knight throws his dag-
ger at what seems to be the voice of Brother Nicholas saying
''*nothing means anything* . . .'' (89), Brother Ivo knows that
he has not only found a true friend, but that he has looked into
the ''darkness at the heart of things'' (89). In risking all to
save the Phoenix, he is, as David Cowart says, ''like the Phoenix, reborn from his own ashes,''[6] and he achieves, as Gardner's title suggests, a kind of sainthood.

''The Warden''

In ''The Warden,'' Gardner portrays Herr Vortrab, who,
unlike Brother Ivo, fails to win existential courage, choosing
instead the sterile order of a death-in-life.[7] Vortrab is the chief
guard of a prison in an authoritarian country in eastern Europe
at an indefinite time. In the spirit of Kafka, the prison is a mi-
crocosm of the world, and the Warden is its ''god.'' Vortrab
has always taken his orders from the Warden. But shortly after
the execution of the nihilist and murderer Josef Mallin, the
Warden retreats behind the door of his office and fails to answer Vortrab's questions. Yet the prison must maintain order.
And there are growing irregularities. A cook is murdered. A

dying prisoner, whom a guard named Heller calls the "Professor" and believes innocent, has never been officially sentenced. Using his own ideas of order as his authority, Vortrab begins to make decisions.

Like most of Gardner's protagonists, Vortrab is ultimately confronted with the choice between nihilism (personified by the dead murderer Josef Mallin) and idealism (personified by the dying Professor). Vortrab is tempted by the Professor's notion that unparticled matter permeates and impels all things, and is, finally, "God" (96), transcending death and unifying all being. But, like the nihilistic Mallin, he rejects all metaphysics and repeats the Warden's fall, interpreting the silence beyond the door, while otherwise clinging to a rationalistic view of the universe.

Vortrab's rationalism is severely tested by the death of the Professor. Though Heller is a Jew, he insists that the Professor, a Christian, be given a Christian burial. With the assistance of eleven other orthodox Jews—some of them rabbis—Heller lays the Christian to rest in a seeming parody of Christ and the apostles. Meanwhile Vortrab sees the Warden standing by the grave, his head blown partially away, his hand cradling a revolver. Though Vortrab has known at some level of consciousness that the Warden is dead—that he will never answer the door—he dismisses his vision as fantasy or illusion—and thus dismisses the metaphysics the Professor had affirmed.

Instead of resolving the Christian analogue, however, Gardner ends ironically with a parody of Sartre. Like Sartre—or Gardner's vision of Sartre—Vortrab is perversely rationalistic. When a foolish man tries to sell him an unnamed book (*Being and Nothingness*) sometime later, he throws him out. The book began, Vortrab says, quoting from memory, "*Mod-*

ern thought has made considerable progress by reducing the existent to the series of appearances which manifest it. Its aim was to overcome certain dualisms which have embarrassed philosophy, and to replace them by the singleness of the phenomenon . . ." (119). Vortrab has indeed, at the expense of his spiritual health and happiness, denied the spirit in matter affirmed by the Professor and objectified by the Warden's ghost. Instead, like the Warden, he has retreated into the prison of the self behind the walls of his consciousness, from which he continues to interpret the Warden's silence. With each new regulation that Vortrab introduces, Heller seems more in despair. Vortrab whispers to him, "if Order has value, you and I are the only hope!" (119). But they share a death-in-life—the kind of order that Fred Clumly has before he meets the Sunlight Man.

"John Napper Sailing Through the Universe"

To counterpoint the dark and hopeless vision of "The Warden," Gardner ends "The Midnight Reader" with "John Napper Sailing Through the Universe," one of his sunniest and most affirmative stories. By contrast to the unimaginative Vortrab, trapped in his spiritual prison, the painter John Napper moves in his art from darkness to light, from the "coal pit" at the center of his existence to the bright optimism of sea spray, antic motion, and women among flowers.

Though ostensibly autobiographical, Gardner's first-person narrative borders on the surreal, exaggerating the actions and reactions of both himself and his subject, a close friend as well as the illustrator of *The Sunlight Dialogues*. The character of John Napper is in part a projection of Gardner's ideal artist and human being, and he echoes many of Gardner's extraliterary comments about art and life.

Presenting himself as a character as well as a narrator, Gardner sets the story around 1970 and begins in a reflective and melancholic mode. He recalls his drunken return, with his wife Joan, from a party, and establishes the surreal vision of the story by saying that Joan—also drunk—does not park the car but instead "hangs it up by one fender on the sagging fence" (121).

As Joan helps John to bed, he is burdened with thoughts of age. But as they contemplate Napper's painting of their young daughter Lucy, a "snag in Time" (121), Gardner calls up an image of the "huge old man," with "wild gray long hair" and clothes "that transcended shabbiness . . ." (121). He remembers Napper at university parties in Carbondale, singing ballads, playing the guitar, "full of joy, mad Irish" (122). Then, missing John Napper, Gardner seeks him out in Europe.

Pushing at the boundaries of realism, and projecting aspects of his own vision of existence and art, Gardner establishes a thematic polarity using Paris and London. When Gardner visits Napper's studio in Paris, he sees his apprentice paintings—and discovers a "John Napper" he had never known. The early works "were a shock: dark, furious, intellectual, full of scorn and something suicidal" (124). But before it was too late, Napper had somehow shaken his head at this bleak vision, and jumped back from the "edge of self-destruction. . . . He would make up the world from scratch: Let there be light, a splendid garden" (133). He had discovered what all of Gardner's moral artists discover: that the imagination can redeem, turn a hell into a heaven.

In London, Gardner finds a large seascape on the wall of Napper's studio—a metaphor of Napper's voyage from despair to affirmation, his celebration of the light over the dark. And though he offers affectionate and amused glimpses of Napper drinking and singing, finding everything in life "marvelous," and agreeing ("exactly") with everyone while never changing his idea of the truth, the story is ultimately more about John Gardner and his need for affirmation than it is about John Napper. When Gardner tells Napper that he is "crazy," that he always sees the "best in everything," Napper protests that the good is "*there*," and suddenly looks "young, violent." And when Gardner says again that Napper is "crazy," Napper responds: " 'exactly!' . . . his wide eyes glittering, his smile thrown forward in the darkness like a spear" (134). Though Napper is no saint, he has won, like Gardner's Brother Ivo, the courage of the moral artist to defy chaos and affirm the light.

"Book Two: Tales of Queen Louisa"

Gardner's salute to Napper's creative madness functions as a transition to the literal madness of Queen Louisa, who has indeed turned life into art—but as a defense against reason rather than chaos. Reason is too painful for Queen Louisa to entertain. She cannot accept the reality of her daughter Muriel's "dramatic leaving" (152), and she has retreated into the world of art, where, as James Chandler says in *The Resurrection,* quoting Wallace Stevens, a "great disorder is an order."

Significantly, the relationship of Queen Louisa's madness to Muriel's "dramatic leaving" is only hinted at in the three tales in *The King's Indian:* "Queen Louisa," "King Gregor and the Fool," and "Muriel." Only in a fourth tale, "Trumpeter," dropped from this collection and published in *The Art of Living,* does Gardner say directly that Muriel has died.

"Queen Louisa" is a comic variation on the tale of the frog who becomes a prince. Gardner's Queen Louisa shape-shifts back and forth between a "magnificently beautiful red-headed woman" and an enormous toad with a swamp green torso, wattles, and great, heavy-lidded eyes covered by spectacles. Upon awakening (as a toad) in her royal boudoir Queen Louisa immediately and bizarrely intuits that Tanya, her fourteen-year-old chambermaid, is pregnant, that Tanya is really her missing daughter, Muriel, and that King Gregor is having an affair with the "witch," her lady-in-waiting.

Queen Louisa at once decides to put the lady-in-waiting on trial. But the judges—"sheep" in Queen Louisa's imagination—will not try the "alleged witch" in absentia, and so they move the trial to a monastery, where the "witch" is found hacking at a rose bush while a red hound whimpers at her feet. Giving up on the rose bush, since it blossoms more each time she strikes it, the witch suddenly commands one hundred wolves in monks' robes to surround Queen Louisa—and then delivers a parodic version of Sartre's existential vision: "We're cosmic accidents! . . . Life is gratuitous, it has no meaning till we make one up by our intensity" (151). But then in a final shape-shifting climax, one thousand knights save Queen Louisa, who turns from a "swampgreen" toad into a beautiful redheaded woman, while the red hound turns into King Gregor, the witch into the lady-in-waiting, and the blooming rose bush—symbol of the victory of good over evil—into an ice-covered stick.

Though Queen Louisa is essentially a comic character, the subtext of her daughter's death gives the tale a bittersweet tone. Gardner emphasizes this tragic undercurrent when the queen tells Tanya-Muriel that she should not feel guilty about her "dramatic leaving," even though it provoked King

Gregor's sexual promiscuity—and, by implication, her own mental promiscuity. But Gardner wants to keep sentiment at bay, and, in postmodernist fashion, he ends the tale by calling attention to it as a work of fiction and to himself as the "coachman" who made it possible:

> The boy beside the coachman said: "Isn't this a marvelous tale to be in?"
>
> The coachman, who was silver-haired and wise, gave his nephew a wink. "You barely made it, laddie!" (152).

Gardner narrates "Queen Louisa" from the third-person subjective viewpoint, generating grotesque images through the queen's surreal vision of reality and creating empathy for her dilemma as well as bewildered amusement in the reader. By contrast, he narrates the second tale, "King Gregor and the Fool," from the perspective of a persona who has only a limited knowledge of events and can only speculate on their meaning. Though this creates a complementary shift in tone and rhythm between the stories, it also generates a more detached viewpoint for the reader and, in doing so, replaces the wildly surreal with the more conventionally ironic.

The irony in "King Gregor and the Fool" depends on the reader's recognition of what is invalid about the narrative persona's observations. The narrator picks up where "Queen Louisa" leaves off, and speculates that King Gregor's neglect of Queen Louisa had encouraged Queen Louisa to spend more time as a toad; and Tanya, his alleged daughter, to run away and get pregnant. The narrator reports, too, that King Gregor had become so unhappy with his prating and carping Fool that he suggested to his fellow kings that they behead all the Fools and let the people vote.

Gardner's major focus in the story, however, is on the war between King Gregor and King John. Though their soldiers die on the battlefield and body counts are taken, they have lunch together regularly, and King Gregor confides that he is depressed about his marriage. He is even more depressed, however, when Queen Louisa interrupts his magnificent cavalry charge, saying "you people are all crazy" (165). And when his Fool recites a couplet on the same theme, King Gregor is ready to behead him. The Fool's neck is saved, however, when "Just" King John agrees with the Fool that "the passage is distinctly Biblical. Loosely" (169), thus forcing an end to war, since it is clearly in conflict with Biblical teachings.

In "Muriel," Gardner shifts from a parody of war to what Jeff Henderson calls a "parable of social revolution," noting that the name "Tanya" alludes to Patricia Hearst—called "Tania" by the Symbionese Liberation Army during her abduction.[8] As in "Queen Louisa," Gardner starts with an omniscient viewpoint and then gradually adopts the language and perspective of the protagonist: Tanya-Muriel. And again, as in "King Gregor and the Fool," the tale begins where the previous tale ends. At first the newly born Tanya-Muriel spends her time trying on dresses and deciphering love verses from chivalrous knights. And she has just decided that "modern poetry" is too complicated when she is bounced out of her carriage in the middle of the dark wood, where Vrokror, her evil lover and father of her unborn child, is lurking.

When she regains consciousness, however, she is disappointed to find that she is not in Vrokror's lair but in a church basement, where her peasant friends insist she tell them about life at court. Though she does so, her thoughts soon shift to Vrokror, and Gardner again parodies the imagery and style of Poe, ending with a comic self-portrait, mirroring his "prematurely gray" hair, the cast in his left eye, and other details. But though Tanya loves Vrokror, she foils his plot to entrap

Queen Louisa—and Vrokror flees to a nearby mountain, leaving Tanya behind. (He returns, in ''Trumpeter,'' to marry her.)

It is axiomatic, of course, that comic incongruities lose their power when eccentric characters and situations become familiar and normative, as they do in the tales that follow ''Queen Louisa.'' But it is also clear that Gardner's imagination was more deeply stimulated by Queen Louisa's comically grotesque character than it was by the characters of either King Gregor or Muriel, who take the center of their tales, leaving Queen Louisa at the side. Indeed, ''Queen Louisa'' is perhaps the most widely read of Gardner's short fictions, since it has been reprinted for some time in two popular anthologies of fiction,[9] as an engaging and amusing example of contemporary fabulation.

''The King's Indian: A Tale''

A novella divided into chapters, ''The King's Indian'' is an elaborate work of metafiction and fabulation. Though the novella was partially inspired by John Barth's literary parodies in *The Sot-Weed Factor* (1960) and *Chimera* (1972), Gardner would later criticize Barth in *On Moral Fiction,* categorizing him as part of a group who ''no longer seek truth, or goodness or beauty, but address their talents to parody, to role-playing . . .'' (54); and who ''may be not so much a group of post-modernists as a gang of absurdists and jubilant nihilists . . .'' (54–55). Casual readers of *On Moral Fiction* have therefore been misled by this and similar comments, and have concluded that Gardner is attacking formal experimentation and asserting that ''moral'' fiction should be ''true'' to reality—in a word, ''realistic.'' But as Donald Greiner observes,

Gardner was "attacking not the joyous flaunting of technique but the trivializing of moral values. . . ."[10]

Gardner was as ambivalent about Barth's vision of existence as he was about Sartre's. The tenor of his remarks in *On Moral Fiction* is anticipated, for example, by those he made five years earlier, in January 1973, when he referred to Barth, along with Donald Barthelme and Kurt Vonnegut Jr. as "cynical" though "technically very good."[11] And it was Barth's technical virtuosity that he was praising in July 1973 when, shortly after completing "The King's Indian," he told Joe David Bellamy, "I think wonderful sandcastles are terrific; I think they're moral. I think they make you a better person much more than a sermon does. I like Barth's funhouse metaphor. I think it's right. Every writer now is lost in the funhouse—and pretty happy with it."[12] That is, Gardner admired the imaginative leaps of Barth's famous metafictional story "Lost in the Funhouse," which inspired him to use the "funhouse" metaphor. But he rejected the Sartrean existentialism of such novels as Barth's *The End of the Road* (1958; rev. ed. 1967). Gardner wanted, instead, to create a "funhouse" that was "moral," since he believed that a fictional experience in a moral funhouse could make "you a better person" than a "sermon" in a church.

The moral funhouse of "The King's Indian" is even more brightly illuminated by Gardner's comment to Bellamy about Barth's *The Sot-Weed Factor,* a parody of the eighteenth-century novel. With this novel in mind, Gardner observes that the supposedly "innovative" use of self-reflexive and disrupted narrative had in fact been anticipated by the novel *Tom Jones* (1749), in which Henry Fielding violates the reader's sense of fictive "reality" by interjecting self-reflexive comments, lightly mocking his characters, and generally reminding the reader of his hovering presence. As Gardner put it, "now everybody is doing Fielding, suddenly tired of the small-minded seriousness of [realistic] novels, their delicate apprehensions, and going instead for big emotions, going for big commitments, or for big jokes. *The Sot-Weed Factor* is, I think, nothing but a big joke. It's a philosophical joke; it might even be argued that it's a philosophical advance. But it ain't like Victor Hugo. You're always aware of a page" (171). Again, Gardner's praise for *The Sot-Weed Factor*, like his praise for Barth's "Lost in the Funhouse," must be seen in the larger context of Gardner's moral vision. Seven months earlier, in December 1972, he told another interviewer, "John Barth is a fabulous technician. *The Sot-Weed Factor* is such a technically perfect book that one wishes it had more feeling, that Barth could love more."[13]

Gardner's reactions to *The Sot-Weed Factor*, however valid—or contradictory—would in fact inspire one of the many parodies in "The King's Indian." As Gardner says, the reader is "always aware of a page" when reading *The Sot-Weed Factor*. Similarly, the reader is always aware of a page when reading "The King's Indian," and it is also, like *The Sot-Weed Factor*, "a big joke," a "tale" whose convoluted plot develops out of a hoax generated by two shipowners: James T. Horner, an allusion to Jacob ("Jake") Horner, the protagonist of *The End of the Road;* and Tobias Cook, an allusion to Ebenezer Cooke, the protagonist of *The Sot-Weed Factor*. Like Ebenezer Cooke, Gardner's protagonist, Jonathan Upchurch, goes on a wild adventure at sea and meets up with an antagonist, Dr. Luther Flint, who appears magically out of nowhere like Barth's Henry Burlingame.[14] And Gardner winks at Barth's *Chimera* and its famous narrator when Jonathan Upchurch rests from telling his tale for a moment, and the listener (his "guest") responds, "What a tale! . . . I swear, all the lightnings of Scheherazade can't hold a candle to it!" (255).

Described as a "crafty old loon with his left eye cocked to the northwest corner of the universe" (197), Upchurch mirrors not only Coleridge's Ancient Mariner but John Gardner himself, including the cast in his left eye, which Herbert Fink exaggerates in his illustration of Gardner as Jonathan Upchurch. While ghosts wander aimlessly as in Coleridge's poem, Upchurch (perhaps dead, perhaps in heaven) sits in a tavern and tells his tale to the enthusiastic guest, while an angel brings them "spirits."

Of a total of twenty-nine chapters in the novella, twenty-two are narrated by Jonathan Upchurch. The other seven chapters (1, 5, 7, 10, 15, 22, and 28) are narrated, in counterpoint to Upchurch's essentially comic tale, by the shadowy persona of "John Gardner," who frames the tale, characterizes Upchurch, and then enters the tale himself, initially disguised as a condemned man in a "dungeon," but finally speaking, unmasked, directly to the reader.[15]

Though Gardner's conflation of literary allusions—to Barth, Poe, Melville, Twain, Faulkner, and others—is almost bewildering, the comic rhetoric of his narrator, Jonathan Upchurch, is compelling and engaging. Using the rhetorical flourishes of the American tall tale and its picaresque heroes, Gardner's narrator (and symbolic alter ego) begins by explaining how, when young and innocent, he got drunk on Nantucket Island and bought a sailboat from pirates who failed to mention they did not own it. After sailing into open seas, Jonathan was rescued by the whaling ship *Jerusalem* headed for the Vanishing Isles. Once on board the ship Jonathan meets—or thinks he meets—Captain Dirge, his daughter Augusta, and other characters who are not what they seem.

Jonathan ultimately discovers, however, that he has sailed beyond reality into fabulation, while Gardner pushes the reader toward comic disbelief in a complex plot filled with shape-shifting characters and identities. The owners of the *Jerusalem,* Horner and Cook, aided by a man named Wilkins, had concocted a story to deceive and embarrass the pompous and gullible Captain Dirge, telling him that a duplicate of the *Jerusalem,* which he had just sailed into port, had been sunk in a maelstrom off the Vanishing Isles. As evidence of this event, they produced a painting of Dr. Luther Flint (cf. Captain Flint of Stevenson's *Treasure Island*), which they claimed was found where the ship sank—but which was hanging simultaneously in Dirge's cabin.

Convinced that the duplicate "ghost" ship sank in a different dimension of time, Captain Dirge immediately planned a voyage to the Vanishing Islands. But when he told his plans to his hero, Dr. Flint, he effectively scuttled his own life. As Jonathan Upchurch finally discovers, Flint—an evil Prospero with a daughter named Miranda—murdered both Dirge and his daughter, replacing Dirge with a Dirge-like puppet, and Augusta with Miranda, and disguising himself as the blind seer Jeremiah.

Flint was assisted in the murders, as well the continuing deception aboard the *Jerusalem,* by Wilkins, who is disguised as Swami Havananda. Though Flint has spent his professional life as a magician hoaxing audiences by staging illusions of supernatural events, he so desperately wants to believe in what Wilkins calls "some holiness past magic" (308) that he ignores all signs of the hoax that inspired the voyage. In the end, Wilkins, bitterly disappointed in Flint, rapes Flint's daughter and kills himself, while Flint experiences spontaneous combustion when Jonathan—supposedly a novice—opens a chess game with a move called "The King's Indian."

In earlier fiction Gardner uses *The Rime of the Ancient Mariner* as a hovering or implied metaphor to organize his emotions and thoughts. In "The King's Indian," the projection of himself as the Ancient Mariner encourages the reader to examine the persona—or implied author—"John Gardner." In doing so, Gardner makes his thinly disguised persona a self-conscious and self-reflexive participant in the narrative. Though Gardner parodies the work of other writers in this novella, his narrative self-consciousness leads him to parody his own work as well.

Having established Jonathan as a double for the Ancient Mariner, Gardner introduces the "albatross" in various comic disguises. At first, Jonathan, hypnotized by Dr. Flint, imagines that the ship is being followed by "an enormous, pigeon-like bird as white as snow" (235); then—under the influence of hallucinogenic mushrooms—he sees an "enormous pigeon or webless boobie," which walks beside him with its wing on his arm (281); then he sees a "huge, partly visible pigeon," which shakes its head in disgust but suggests that "something may come of this queer business yet" (293). And then a "big white bird" saves Jonathan's life through telepathy, before becoming, finally, the "Holy Ghost," who is "disguised as a sea-boobie" and utters the novella's last, obscene, line.

Since, in this comic reversal of Coleridge's symbolism, the variously disguised albatross saves Jonathan's life, he has less need of grace than Miranda Flint, who like her father has been evil all her life. After she is raped and beaten by Wilkins, however, she moves toward atonement. Though her beauty has been badly marred by her experience, Jonathan acknowledges her attractiveness by touching her breast. In doing so, he accidentally plays the role of Coleridge's water snakes—and effects the last of Gardner's comic reversals: "She reached to me suddenly and pulled me to her. 'You're so *wall*-eyed!' she whispered. I saw on her face a wild, unintentional idea. 'Jonathan, I love you,' she whispered. 'You're grotesque' '' (322)—at which point Gardner adds in the margin, ''[She blesses him unaware.]'' And at which point, the lovers feel grace, a wind comes up, and Jonathan tells the crew, including the African novelist James Ngugi and the African-American novelist Charles Johnson, to make some sails; that they are off ''to Illinois the Changeable!'' (323).

Gardner saw Coleridge as a dominant force in the American tradition, and noted especially the influence of *The Rime of the Ancient Mariner* on Poe's *The Narrative of Arthur Gordon Pym,* and two of Melville's masterworks: *Benito Cereno* and *Moby-Dick*. But though he parodies Coleridge throughout ''The King's Indian,'' he indicated that the novella's fundamental conflict arises from the thematic tension between freedom and slavery in all its forms, and that he had developed this theme by alternating between a parody of Poe, who was in favor of slavery, and a parody of Melville, who was opposed to it:

> The opposition of the two views is one of the deep oppositions in the American spirit, and so I copy the way Poe writes and the way Melville writes in my attempt to get at the basic ideas, the American ''problem.'' By using parody, by using Poe against Melville and then commenting on the two of them with the help of Mark Twain, the great literary exponent of the flim-flam man— Jonathan Upchurch as trickster—you get the whole spectrum of American opinion on freedom and responsibility. . . . I definitely want the voices to be heard.[16]

But though the voices of Poe, Melville, and Twain are heard, the dialectic on freedom vs. slavery is almost lost in the echoes of other writers.

In developing the parodies, Gardner assumes the reader is not only familiar with *Moby-Dick, Benito Cereno,* and *The Adventures of Huckleberry Finn,* but also with Poe's *The Narrative of Arthur Gordon Pym,* a little-read work. Consequently, some readers miss the fundamental irony of Gardner's narrative, since he not only parallels the key actions of Poe's novel but puns on Poe's language as well. For example: Jonathan, like Pym, is rescued by a whaler; he echoes Pym's seabirds ("Tekeli-li!") when he yells "Tack alee" at the ship's crew; and his rescue from the ship's rigging echoes the moment in which Pym is saved from falling off a cliff.[17]

Like *Arthur Gordon Pym, Moby-Dick* sails in metaphysical seas, and Gardner compares Captain Dirge to Ahab, while echoing two of Melville's chapters: "The Lee Shore" and, in more detail, "The Mast-Head," where Ishmael warns a sailor assigned to the crow's nest not to blend his vision of waves and thoughts. But Jonathan is just that kind of unwary and introspective sailor, and he directly echoes Ishmael's warning and imagery: "It was as if I had lost identity, become one with the mystic ocean at my feet, image of the deep-blue bottomless soul that pervades all mankind and nature like Cranmer's ashes" (237).[18]

As Gardner later indicated, "The King's Indian" explores slavery in relation to Melville and other writers. Echoing *Benito Cereno,* for example, Jonathan learns that there are twenty-five black slaves below deck and they later participate in a mutiny. Echoing Twain's *Huckleberry Finn,* Jonathan reacts to Captain Dirge's appearance with Huck's voice and style: "It gave me such creeps and crawls along my spine I blame near bolted" (247–48). And later, Miranda Flint refers to Jonathan's black companion, James Ngugi, as his "Nigger Jim" (318), implying of course that Jonathan is "Huck."

But Jonathan is also like Isaac McCaslin, the protagonist of Faulkner's "The Bear" in *Go Down, Moses,* which explores the impact of slavery in even greater depth. When Jonathan first discovers the slaves, he thinks immediately of a "butchered bear in van Klug's front window—hung upside down, like Peter on the cross . . ." (218); then, shortly after, he hears the slaves singing *Go-down-Moziz* (239). And when the *Jerusalem* sails below the equator, Jonathan discovers the constellation of the "Great Bear had vanished" (232); that it has been replaced by the "Captain," who looms up "like a great, black, hunchbacked bear . . ." (255), and overwhelms Jonathan with a sense of lost connection when he discovers that a slave has been mistaken for him and murdered: " '*Guilty!*' I thought. All poor miserable mankind, *guilty!* Pitifully tilting up grandiose ikons of the bears they slaughter or the corn they chop, and praying to the ikons in terror and anguish: 'O Lord, Dread Ruler of Life and Death—' (Aye, there's the story of yer obstinate survival of ancient beliefs! Love, sir! The love of a man and bear and windblown wheatfields; love and the misery of killers!)'' (277). Guilt isolates Jonathan metaphysically from his connection with what Coleridge called the "One Life" and symbolized with the albatross and the water snakes. But since Gardner has repeatedly parodied the symbolism of the albatross ("enormous pigeon," "sea-boobie," the "Holy Ghost") he can no longer use the symbolism as a metaphor of his protagonist's lost grace. He therefore adopts Faulkner's bear as a symbol of connection (and, it should be noted, repeats this symbolism in *October Light*).

Given the centrality of Coleridge's poem to Gardner's vision, his parody of the Mariner's experience of guilt and redemption is in effect self-parody, and it marks Gardner's

movement toward a more consistently self-conscious stance
as narrator. This self-consciousness—so much a part of the
postmodernist stories of Barth, Ronald Suckenick, and others—led Gardner in turn toward a progressively more autobiographical, undisguised, and melancholic persona which
competes with the comic hyperbole of Jonathan Upchurch. As
if apologizing for playing postmodernist games, Gardner's
persona defends, in a gloomy voice, the metafiction and fabulation which Jonathan Upchurch is creating.

In the seven chapters which frame Jonathan Upchurch's
narrative, Jonathan and the guest initially pause to comment
on the tale being told. But in chapters 5, 10, and 22, the shadowy persona of "John Gardner" speaks from a dungeon,
where, in a gloomy counterpoint to Jonathan Upchurch's fabulation, he tells his own guest, identified as the "Inspector,"
about art: "Let us speak of great works of art, or even foolish
ones; brute objects decayed as old mountains, eternal in-
stants.—But time's too short for that, I agree with you. Tack
alee, then, mate, away from the maelstrom, away from the
Coal-pocket, upward in all directions, home to Visions!"
(215–15). When Gardner's persona directs their attention
away from the nihilism of the "Coal-pocket" toward the fabulation in progress, however, the inspector asks if he is serious—to which Gardner's persona responds affirmatively, as
Gardner did in interviews, "Serious in the manner of a sand
castle . . ." (215).

In chapter 22, Gardner gives up the "dungeon" persona
entirely and speaks directly—though not by name—of his dying friend Nicholas Vergette, the artist to whom he dedicated
the volume in which the novella appears. Whereas Flint plays
cynical "tricks on the world" (like John Barth, Gardner suggests) Gardner's friend (whom he later memorialized in the

poem "Nicholas Vergette: 1923–1974") gives the last of his life to painting the artistic truth of a "pale yellow lemon on a field of white" (294).

In counterpointing the tragic vision of his "dungeon" persona against the comic vision of Jonathan Upchurch, Gardner clearly wishes to establish the moral significance of his fabulation—or "sand castle." But the allusion to his dying friend threatens the ironic tone of his fabulation, and it anticipates the subjective voice of the framing chapter (28), where Gardner alludes first to Barth's influential metafiction, "Lost in the Funhouse," then to Barth's equally influential essay, "The Literature of Exhaustion," and then, in an implied contrast, to Vergette's moral art:

> This house we're in is a strange one, reader—house or old trunk or circus tent—and it's one I hope you find congenial, sufficiently gewgawed and cluttered but not unduly snug. Take my word, in any case, that I haven't built it as a cynical trick, one more bad joke of exhausted art. The sculptor-turned-painter that I mentioned before is an actual artist, with a name I could name, and what I said of him is true. . . . And this book, this book is no child's top either—though I write, more than usual, filled with doubts. Not a toy but a queer, cranky monument, a collage: a celebration of all literature and life; an environmental sculpture, a funeral crypt. (316)

As Gardner says, he wrote "The King's Indian" while, "more than usual, filled with doubts." Though he originally intended "The King's Indian" to be a metafiction—a fiction about fiction—life intruded in the person of Nicholas Vergette. Gardner partially sublimates his grief at Vergette's imminent death in the tragic vision of the "dungeon" persona, who defends the fabulation. But finally, in a moment which Gardner later regretted,[19] he pushes his persona aside and speaks directly to his readers, implicitly assuring them that his fiction is not, like Barth's, "a cynical trick, one more bad joke of exhausted art." This disclaimer, however, did not work: more than one reviewer linked Gardner to Barth, and saw no difference between them—one of the reasons, perhaps, that Gardner so insistently criticized Barth's postmodernism and "nihilism" in *On Moral Fiction.*

Reviewers had difficulty evaluating the novella and the shorter tales. Gardner had created the literary equivalent of jazz improvisation. To appreciate the improvisation, readers had to know the original work, and not all of Gardner's reviewers were either ready or willing, especially under a deadline, to have the metafictional experience. There were, however, notable exceptions: Doris Grumbach wrote in *The New Republic* that the collection was "close to perfection in its invention and imagination,"[20] while George Levine wrote in *Partisan Review* that "The King's Indian" was, apart from *Grendel,* perhaps Gardner's finest work, and that together they illustrated Gardner's faith that narrative was "the way to say yes to life."[21] But most reviewers praised the more realistic stories—"Pastoral Care" and "John Napper Sailing Through the Universe"—and expressed the hope that Gardner would abandon fabulation and/or metafiction and return to more traditional narratives.

As *October Light* reveals, however, Gardner's imagination was stimulated by literary counterpoint and parody, and he was not ready to capitulate.

NOTES

1. Marshall Harvey, "Where Philosophy and Fiction Meet: An Interview with John Gardner," *Chicago Review* 29 (Spring 1978): 82.

2. John Gardner and Lennis Dunlap, eds., *The Forms of Fiction* (New York: Random House, 1962) 30.

Notes

3. John Gardner, *The King's Indian: Stories and Tales* (New York: Knopf, 1974) 9. Parenthetical page references in the text are to this edition.

4. Jeff Henderson, *John Gardner: A Study of the Short Fiction* (Boston: Twayne, 1990) 22.

5. Henderson 23.

6. David Cowart, *Arches and Light: The Fiction of John Gardner* (Carbondale: Southern Illinois University Press, 1983) 84–85.

7. For an account of the story's genesis, see Henderson 25–30, 122–24.

8. Henderson 37.

9. "Queen Louisa" appears, with commentary, in *Superfiction, or The American Story Transformed: An Anthology,* ed. Joe David Bellamy (New York: Vintage, 1975) 157–72; and *Studies in Fiction,* ed. Blaze O. Bonazza, Emil Roy, and Sandra Roy, 3rd. ed. (New York: Harper & Row, 1982) 362–69.

10. Donald J. Greiner, "Sailing Through *The King's Indian* with John Gardner and His Friends," *John Gardner: Critical Perspectives,* ed. Robert A. Morace and Kathryn VanSpanckeren (Carbondale: Southern Illinois University Press, 1982) 78.

11. Tony Davis, "John Gardner Heroes Include Achilles, Aeneas, Beowulf, Hector. . . ." *Daily Northwestern* 31 Jan. 1973: 3.

12. Joe David Bellamy and Pat Ensworth, "Interview with John Gardner," *The New Fiction: Interview with Innovative American Writers,* ed. Joe David Bellamy (Urbana: University of Illinois Press, 1974) 192.

13. Richard Natale, "John Gardner: 'Great Age of the Novel is Returning,' " *Women's Wear Daily* 8 Dec. 1972: 16.

14. See Elzbieta Foeller, "John Gardner's Tale: 'The King's Indian' as a Fabulation Based on the 19th-Century Literary Tradition," *Traditions in the Twentieth Century American Literature,* ed. Marta Sienicka (Poznan, Poland: Adam Mickiewicz University, 1981) 84ff.

15. See Robert A. Morace, "The Moral Structure of John Gardner's 'The King's Indian,' " *Midwest Quarterly* 24 (Summer 1983): 390–99.

16. Heide Ziegler, "John Gardner," *The Radical Imagination and the Liberal Tradition: Interviews with English and American Authors,* ed. Heide Ziegler and Christopher Bigsby (London: Junction Books, 1982) 145–46.

17. For more detailed studies of these and other parallels, see Gregory L. Morris, *A World of Order and Light: The Fiction of John Gardner* (Athens: University of Georgia Press, 1984) 243–44; and Per Winther, *The Art of John Gardner: Instruction and Exploration* (Albany: State University of New York Press, 1992) 118–23, 125–26, 129–30.

18. See the relevant passage in Herman Melville, *Moby-Dick* (Indianapolis: Bobbs-Merrill, 1964) 214.

19. Per Winther, "An Interview with John Gardner," *English Studies* 62 (Dec. 1981): 512.

Understanding John Gardner

20. Doris Grumbach, ''Fine Print,'' *New Republic* 21 Dec. 1974: 24.
21. George Levine, ''The Name of the Game,'' *Partisan Review* 42 (Spring 1975): 296.

CHAPTER SIX

October Light

*O*ctober Light (1976), illustrated by Elaine Raphael and Don Bolognese, tells of the battle between James L. Page and his sister Sally Page Abbott. It is the October of their lives as well as of the year. James is seventy-two, Sally is eighty. James has lost his youngest son Ethan to a fall from a barn, his eldest son Richard to a suicide by hanging, and his wife, Ariah, to cancer; only his daughter Virginia (''Ginny'') survives. Sally, a widow, had a childless though happy marriage to Horace Abbott, a dentist, who left her a decent inheritance. But she frittered the inheritance away in an antique business and has come to live with James on his dairy farm near Bennington, Vermont.

Sally's first big mistake upon moving into James's house was to bring a TV set. James had watched it for two weeks in growing outrage at its ''monstrously obscene games of greed,'' its ''leering glittering-toothed monsters of ceremonies,'' its ''endless simpering dramas''; and he had loaded his shotgun and blown the screen ''to hell, right back where it come from.''[1] Then, a week or so later, infuriated at her TV-inspired advocacy of such outrageous notions as the ''Equal Rights Amendment,'' ''agribusiness,'' and ''Amnesty for the War Resisters,'' James had chased Sally (as in a cartoon) upstairs with a ''fireplace log'' and locked her bedroom door. When he had relented and said she could come out, she had refused—and gone on an apparent hunger strike.

By isolating Sally in her bedroom, apart from her friends and James, Gardner challenges his own narrative ingenuity.

He solves the problem at least partially by situating Sally's bedroom next to the house's only bathroom. After using the bathroom the guests stop to talk to Sally through her bedroom door, while much of the time Ginny's husband, Lewis Hicks, paints a nearby closet door and quietly observes. (Fortunately, too, Sally has a second door, which leads to the attic where James has stored twelve bushels of apples. Though ostensibly on a hunger strike, she feeds on the apples.)

As in *Grendel* and *The King's Indian,* Gardner explores the failure of communication. He introduces the same metaphor when Sally observes that "people had all those languages *not* to be understood. They were castle walls" (45–46). And he makes the reader keenly aware of language by accentuating the Vermont dialect. James says "cah" for "car," and he tells his daughter, Ginny (whom he calls "sweet-hot") that "wintah's just around the cohnah" (189), and that he had "used the aht of pahsuasion" (192) when he chased her aunt up the stairs with a log. And after James loses his false teeth in an almost fatal accident, his grotesque enunciation resembles the "Down East" humor of nineteenth-century New England, playing against the tragic events of his past and present, and distancing the reader from his suffering.

James's character reflects Gardner's satirical response to social and political values. In addition to television, James hates foreign cars, the state of California, Coca-Cola, "store-bought ice cream" (12), and the commercialization of Christmas. And, like his daughter, Ginny, he is offended by the commercial exploitation of the Bicentennial of 1976.[2] A conservative Republican, James blames the Democrats for society's problems. He is proud to have been born on the fourth of July, and he is steeped in the history and heroes of the American Revolution. In addition to heading each chapter with a descriptive caption, Gardner includes epigraphs taken from the writings of revolutionary heroes like Charles Biddle, John Dickinson, Benjamin Franklin, John Adams, and George Washington. But though James is, as the caption to chapter 1 indicates, a "Patriot," he has no illusions about the human frailties of these heroes, and he is quick to point out the political duplicity of Sam Adams, the hysterical rages of George Washington, the eccentricities of Benjamin Franklin, the drunkenness of Ethan Allan.

Sally, by contrast to James, is a liberal Democrat. But though she is concerned about women's rights and opportunities, she is essentially apolitical and slow to judge. Thus, unlike the hardheaded James, she is vulnerable to the cynical art and vision of *The Smugglers of Lost Souls' Rock*—the novel left in her room by Ginny's son, Dickie, who retrieved it from the hog pen where James had thrown it. Gardner repeatedly said that "life follows fiction," and argued the case formally in *On Moral Fiction*. He objectifies this thesis by showing Sally's reaction to a morally bankrupt novel. Sally knows *The Smugglers* is trash the minute she reads the blurb—which Gardner obviously enjoyed writing—on the back cover: *"Blows the lid off marijuana smuggling, fashionable gang-bangs, and the much-sentimentalized world of the middle-aged Flower Child. A sick book, as sick and evil as life in America . . ."* (15). But despite her better judgment, and even though pages are missing, she begins to read the novel, acknowledging that she is wasting her time, yet curious about the fate of the characters.

By focusing on the naive responses of a "good" character to a "bad" novel, and by reprinting the text of the book to which she responds, Gardner creates an ironic and often comic disparity between Sally's reaction and the reader's reaction. In effect, *The Smugglers of Lost Souls' Rock* becomes a second character in Sally's bedroom, and Gardner is as much interested in Sally's interaction with the novel as he is in the novel itself.[3] Though the novel is filled with grotesque cliches of character, action, and idea, it engages Sally in a mental and emotional dialogue from which she periodically departs to address the almost palpable spirit of her late husband, Horace, who read only serious literature and would not, she knows, approve.

Unlike James, whose emotions are "locked," as Gardner's pastoral metaphor suggests, Sally is open to fiction as well as to life, and she is by turns irritated and amused as she begins the novel and discovers that its protagonist, Peter Wagner, is hanging by his fingertips from the Golden Gate Bridge and about to commit suicide. Her reaction to his desperate (though comic) character immediately introduces Gardner's counterpoint between the novel she is reading and the life she is living. Though she laughs at Wagner's ironic comments, she is offended by the novel's callous attitude toward suicide, since she immediately compares Wagner's actions to the suicide of James's son Richard. But soon, though she knows better, she is drawn into the novel, "becoming herself more wry, more wearily disgusted with the world—not only with her own but with the whole 'universe,' as the book kept saying . . ." (21).

The plot of *The Smugglers* is as outrageous as Gardner (with the assistance of his wife Joan) could make it. Wagner drops into the sea near the *Indomitable*, a boat sneaking marijuana into San Francisco. The boat is captained by Johann Fist, a ruthless existentialist whose name suggests his Faustian character, and who has clearly lost his soul. When Captain Fist learns that Wagner (named after Faust's servant) can run a boat, he saves him from being shocked to death by the electric eels which have been wired together by the ship's engineer, Mr. Nit, an admirer of Benjamin Franklin's scientific experiments.

In the developing counterpoint, Sally immediately identifies Mr. Nit with Ginny's mechanically adept husband, Lewis Hicks, and Captain Fist with her autocratic brother, James, while she compares herself wistfully to the novel's sexually voracious heroine Jane, "a living *Playboy* foldout" (99), who writes cheerful and highly selective travel letters home to her mother. But Sally has no frame of reference for Dr. John F. Alkahest, an elderly paraplegic (and former "brain surgeon") who was riding on a Coast Guard cutter near the point where Wagner hit the water. A Gothic caricature, he is driven mad by the smell of the marijuana from the *Indomitable,* and his quest for the drug provides *The Smugglers* with a subplot.

In contrast to the satanic and morbid figure of Dr. Alkahest—named after alchemy's "universal solvent"—Wagner is whimsically identified with Christ.[4] He is thirty-three years old, repeatedly associated with epithets like "Jesus" or "Christ," called "savior" by the crew, and linked to the Christian symbol of the fish when Jane asks him if he is a "Pisces."

Wagner observes that "all life is a boring novel" when he jumps from the bridge. Ironically, his apparent inspiration for this metaphor is Gardner's novella "The King's Indian," which Wagner leaves behind in a car near the bridge, and which comes to mind after he is rescued from the water—and suddenly realizes that his rescue had all "happened in some novel he'd read about a hoax" (84). Since Sally has not read "The King's Indian," Gardner clearly intends the allusion as a self-reflexive irony, and he turns the irony into an elaborate pun by introducing an "Indian" as a crew member of the *Militant*, captained by Luther Santisillia, an elegant black man with a machine gun who would have been a "king if this were Africa . . ." (158). Together, the "king" and his "Indian," assisted by a black radical named "Dancer," take over the *Indomitable*.

Despite the gaps in the text of *The Smugglers*, it remains an independent, or freestanding, comic novel, with its own internal counterpoint and thematic tensions. Though most of the characters mock traditional ideals and values, some are affirmative in thought and action. And though the novel has a negative impact on Sally's attitude toward the world, it also has a positive impact, which contributes to its incoherence as satire or parody when read in the context of the frame novel.[5]

Sally is annoyed by *The Smugglers* because "by accident it came close enough to life to remind her of it, and life was, Lord knew, a sad business" (170). That is to say, her inept author (Gardner as parodist) has reminded her of fiction's moral potential; momentarily inspired, she becomes her own "shaper," creating an emotionally true—or "moral"—fiction "that might have been a memory except that it was nothing she'd seen, merely a construction built of love like a mother's and the little she knew—those and the novel, which had triggered her gloomy mood" (170). And in this mood, she imagines a brief scene in which Richard, shortly before his death, meets his lost love, the Flynn girl.

Significantly, in a radical change of tone, Gardner counterpoints Sally's "moral" fiction in *October Light* with a moral fiction in *The Smugglers*, where he momentarily gives up his ironic stance and creates an emotionally "true," even loving, portrait of Pearl, the young black woman who works for Dr. Alkahest. Gardner later accounted for this change of tone by indicating that he "started to get very bored with [the novel] and then I invented the character Pearl. She carried me through the rest of it. You finally can't really write about people who aren't people. . . . After you've gone for a while with characters like Peter Wagner, you want to go on to a real person. Like Pearl. It was very strange to me though, because I hadn't planned her."[6] But in creating a "real person" like Pearl, Gardner shifts from cartoon detachment to emotional engagement. In a pointed contrast to Dr. Alkahest's grotesque fantasies about Pearl—the victim of a rape—Gardner reveals how Pearl's trauma has made her afraid of all men, and therefore hostile and potentially exploitive. And moving still further toward a "moral" fiction within a cartoon fiction, he alludes to the contemporary rape trial of Joan Little—an event which makes Pearl "furious and afraid, sometimes violently sick" (172). Ultimately, however, Pearl clings to her Christian faith, resists the temptation to steal a large sum of money from Alkahest, and affirms her humanity.

Gardner uses Pearl's moral fiction to introduce the "bear," or beast, motif in *The Smugglers* and establish a counterpoint to Sally's world, where the motif is pervasive. Sally realizes, in response to Pearl's character, that anyone can lapse into the "mindless bestiality of things," and that, counterpointing Sally's uncle Ira, "one had to be a kind of mad hero, like Peter Wagner's old uncle with the snowplow, to go it alone, and even he had been a destroyer—though not from bestiality" (332). Wagner's uncle Mort had injured one or more people in a car while trying to dig them out of a snowbank, and he is, like Sally's uncle Ira, compared to a bear. But Uncle Ira lived like a beast and died like a beast when he shot himself in the woods. Uncle Mort, by contrast, tried to be a complete human being, and though he may have seemed like a "clown or a bear" (273) trying to "imitate the acrobats" (272) in Gardner's metaphorical circus, he nevertheless transcended "mindless bestiality," just as James does in his symbolic confrontation with an old bear in the final moments of the novel.

Sally associates her uncle Ira's suicide with her nephew Richard's suicide—and both, in turn, with her husband's sudden death from a heart attack. In reading about Wagner's attempts at suicide, she feels an "undertow of anxiety" (103), and in a scene reminiscent of Henry Soames's traumatic reaction to Simon Bale's death in *Nickel Mountain,* she relives her discovery of Horace's corpse on Halloween night twenty years before. Again, she hears the needle stuck on his gramophone, and she knows that she is about to see, with overwhelming clarity, the vision of her husband sitting in his chair, with his mouth

> forming an O as if of slight surprise, and she would cry out and run to him. . . . Every line in the room was as sharp as a razor cut—books, glass-topped table, hat-rack by the door—and for an instant it seems there was a smell, exaggerated by memory but elusive as ever. Someone had been there, someone from her past, perhaps her childhood. All this she had told the police, later, going over it and over it in meticulous detail. "What did it smell like?" "I don't know. The woods," she said. "Decaying leaves. Like a zoo." (104)

This scene—pivotal in the novel—has a compelling *energeia,* which, citing Aristotle, Gardner defines in *The Art of Fiction* as "the actualization of the potential which exists in character and situation."[7] The reader wants to know *why* Horace had the heart attack, *who* was in the room, and *what* caused the lingering smell. These questions generate what

Gardner calls "profluence": the reader anticipates "a causally related sequence of events" and "casts forward to later pages, wondering what will come about and how. It is this casting forward that draws us from paragraph to paragraph and chapter to chapter" (55). In *October Light,* however, Gardner disrupts the profluence—the "casting forward"—by quoting from *The Smugglers of Lost Souls' Rock* and showing Sally's reactions to it. Indeed, some readers are so caught up by the profluence of Sally's "real" world that they resist the interruptions created by the interpolated text of the novel she reads. In doing so, they inevitably ignore the thematic counterpoint that Gardner develops between the two novels.

Gardner repeatedly alludes to the mystery of Horace's death, hinting that "Uncle Ira" is the key to that mystery, and linking the developing perceptions about death, guilt, and spiritual connectedness to the developing motif of a "bear." Sally reflects that Uncle Ira was "not exactly human—he even smelled like an animal—as if his mother'd been brought low by a bear" (136). And James's daughter, Ginny, remembers how Richard had gone to a Halloween party dressed as Uncle Ira, wearing a beard, white hair, and, significantly, Uncle Ira's bear-smelling coat. Even James was amused at Richard's costume—but, as James later discovers, the costume had scared Uncle Horace to death and Richard's guilt had led him to suicide.

James had blamed Richard for the death of little Ethan, who had climbed the ladder that Richard had left propped against the roof of the barn. But Richard blamed himself even more, and after his uncle Horace's death, the burden of guilt was too great for him to bear: he began to drink, finally hanging himself after James confronted him about his behavior. James blamed himself for Richard's suicide, which he interpreted as a vendetta against him. Though Ariah knew the facts of Horace's death, Richard swore her to secrecy, and even when dying of cancer, she would not tell James the truth, since she could forgive neither James nor herself for Richard's death.

Wounded by guilt, emotionally frozen, James repeatedly associates bears with the supernatural, which is ironic, since he does not really believe "that bears are visitors from another world . . . or even, with his whole heart and mind, Resurrection" (13). But when he thinks of how Ariah would react to his battle with Sally, he can hear her saying, "Oh James, James," since "his anger was foolishness. . . . All life was foolishness, a witless bear exploring, poking through woods" (14). Fortunately, when he does confront life in the form of a witless bear at the climactic moment of the novel, he imitates Faulkner's idealistic hunter Isaac McCaslin, not Coleridge's Ancient Mariner, and fails to shoot it.

But though Gardner uses Faulkner's "The Bear" ironically (as in "The King's Indian") to objectify the theme of spiritual connectedness, he anticipates and counterpoints this theme in *October Light* by introducing, without irony, allusions to Matthew Arnold's "Dover Beach" and William Wordsworth's "Tintern Abbey." Again, his comments in *On Moral Fiction* offer an illuminating gloss: " 'God' became, for educated people, a hard word to swear by. Nevertheless, there was 'something,' though it might be no more than (as for Arnold) human love. One got from mountains, beautiful lakes, sometimes panthers, and most often from 'the sad music of humanity,' a general sense of, as Wordsworth expressed it, '. . . something far more deeply interfused. . . .' "[8] Gardner's character Estelle Parks—a retired English teacher—sees literature in these quasi-religious terms. One of Gardner's "saintly intercessors,"[9] Estelle introduces a long quotation from "Tintern Abbey" and later, "as if a party to her thought" (235) about her late husband, Ferris, she hears Ruth Thomas recite "Dover Beach," with its affirmation of human love as the only truth.

Estelle and Ruth are important—though minor—characters who enrich the novel's tone and atmosphere, and allow Gardner to transcend the essential claustrophobia of Sally's isolation and James's narrow perspective. As if writing a scene for a stage comedy, Gardner introduces Ruth and other minor characters as they come into James's house through the kitchen door. Unbeknownst to James, Estelle has invited them to an impromptu party, hoping to draw Sally out of her room. James fumes as Ruth enters, followed by her grandchildren and her husband Ed, a jolly man with a heart condition, who is on her mind when she recites "Dover Beach" and, later— with contradictory tears—a comic poem, "The Bear," which Gardner reprinted in *A Child's Bestiary* (1977). And James is even more irritated at the arrival of Sally's minister, Lane Walker, who, along with a visiting friend, Father Rafe Hernandez, introduces questions of race, religion, and faith. They are followed by Dr. Phelps, his granddaughter Margie, and Estelle's nephew Terence, who plays the French horn in a woodwind quintet with Margie—and later develops a long interior monologue on the esthetic significance of the Tippet Sonata for Four Horns, in a section which Gardner titles "Terence on Pure and Subservient Art" (363).

In counterpoint to the levity in the kitchen, Gardner introduces a Gothic atmosphere already anticipated by the motif of the bear. Though tempted by the arrival of her friends, Sally remains in her room, talking through the door—to Father Hernandez, to Ruth—and then, having dozed off, she awakens

Understanding John Gardner

to what she thinks is Horace's voice. Unnerved by the experience, she looks outside and has a troubling vision: ''Out by the mailbox, standing perfectly still, there was an old, old man in a long, dark coat, bearded like a rabbi'' (230). When she cleans her glasses and looks again, however, he is gone. Was it a ghost? an hallucination? or someone dressed for Halloween?

Gardner never answers the question: Sally only knows that she may have seen a ghost, and though she wants to believe in ghosts, she is afraid of them. Consequently, when she asks Reverend Walker (through the door) if he believes in ghosts, she feels patronized when he jokes that he believes in the ''Holy Ghost,'' and then gives her an impromptu ''sermon'' on evolution, starting with the paradox that the ''apes descended from human beings'' (243), and elaborating Gardner's thematic concern—here as in *Grendel*—with spiritual connectedness.

Gardner partially resolves the themes and actions of *October Light* by parodying two of his favorite novelists: John Fowles and, more significantly and climactically, William Faulkner. In ''The King's Indian,'' Gardner interjects himself as a persona who observes the main action and makes progressively more self-revealing comments. In *October Light,* he is even more directly self-reflexive, imitating the end of *The French Lieutenant's Woman* (1969), where John Fowles enters his novel as a ''bearded man'' and stares at his protagonist Charles Smithson, who concludes that the bearded man is ''decidedly unpleasant.'' James Page has a similar response when Gardner, who praises Fowles's ''self-consciousness'' in *On Moral Fiction* (96), enters *October Light* as an unnamed ''bearded'' man.

After James, still in a rage at Estelle's maneuver, sits down at Merton's Hideaway with his old friends—Sam Frost,

Bill Partridge, and Henry Stumpchurch—he notices three men sitting with two women, two blond teenagers, and a baby in a high chair. Studying the three men, James concludes that one is a local teacher and that the other two are writers, though he does not know their names. In fact, one of the unnamed writers is Nicholas Delbanco and the other is John Gardner, who is seen by James, in notably unflattering terms, as having "brittle gray hair to his shoulders and a big gray beard. He had a sagging, red face and huge dark bags under his eyes, though he didn't look old, maybe fifty. . . . He flourished a pipe, waving it, pointing it, and he talked somewhat louder than the others, feeling his martinis" (289).

Like Fowles's protagonist, James is unsettled when he realizes the bearded man is "staring at him" (290). In *The Sunlight Dialogues,* Millie Hodge realizes, "briefly, that she was merely a character in an endless, meaningless novel. . . ."[10] Unlike Millie, however, James never realizes he is a fictional character, only that he feels "exposed, the whole room mysteriously unsafe" when, upon leaving the tavern, the bearded man pauses as if "about to turn and look back, straight at him; but if that was what was in the man's mind he thought better of it—or in his drunkenness forgot it—and went out" (296). Since James's fictional existence depends on a drunken creator with wavering attention, it is ironic that he survives as a character, particularly since he never identifies his creator, just as Charles Smithson never identifies Fowles in *The French Lieutenant's Woman.*

Though James has not read *The Smugglers,* Gardner uses his reactions to Merton's TV in counterpointing and integrating the novel with *October Light.* James had bought *The Smugglers* because its cover said it was a "comic blockbuster," but he quickly decided it was "pure hogslop, same as TV" (296), and threw it—unread—into the pigsty. The ironic significance of what he sees on Merton's TV set is, therefore, restricted to the reader's perception. Unaware of Pearl's character in *The Smugglers,* for example, James sees that a "Negro girl was taking a shower," and he asks himself, "did advertising like that cause rapes?" (301–2). And unaware that the ending of *The Smugglers* parodies the TV show "Star Trek," James sees, without recognition, a hovering spaceship and "a man with pointed ears" (305)—that is, an image of the show's "Vulcan" character, Mr. Spock.

Gardner's allusion to "Star Trek" has thematic as well as comic relevance. He is parodying the show's repeated use of mechanical redemption—science fiction's deus ex machina— when the characters are mortally threatened, and frantically request that they be transported—or "beamed"—to the spaceship. Unlike James, Sally obviously knows the show, and is thus completely disgusted when a spaceship suddenly appears above Jane and Peter at the end of *The Smugglers,* and Peter cries out, "Save us! . . . We're innocent! Beam us up!" (400).

Ultimately, Gardner counterpoints this parody of "Star Trek" with a climactic parody of "The Bear" in similarly cartoonlike images. When Sally sees that James has rigged a shotgun so that it points at her door, she balances a half-full crate of apples on top of the door and leaves it invitingly ajar. But Ginny is the victim. James is instead saved by an apple tree when he lands in it (cartoonlike) after he misses a corner on his way home, drunk, from Merton's, and watches his uninsured truck crash and burn below him on the mountain side. In the real world, James's character would elicit sympathy. But characteristically, Gardner distances the reader by pushing James's character still further toward the comic grotesque: Beside himself with rage, James chases the people out of his house with a shotgun, and, having lost his teeth as well as his truck in the accident, he yells with comically distorted enunciation, ''Nobodyth thtayin, . . . Partyth ovah!'' (313).

But in another of Gardner's ironic parallels, James's clownlike actions shock Ed Thomas into a heart attack, just as Richard's clownlike actions shocked Horace Abbott into a heart attack twenty years before. James, guilt-ridden and ashamed, clearly feels less than human as he enters Ed's hospital room. Instead of recriminations, however, Ed delivers a pastoral elegy, which Gardner entitles ''Ed's Song.'' Ruth Thomas thinks of her husband ''as a bear'' (34), and he symbolically incarnates the novel's metaphorical bear. Articulating the significance of spiritual connectedness, he expresses regret that this is the last October he will experience winter's locking of the earth, and that he will not see the spring. But he also regrets that he won't see the elections on TV. And well aware of James's attitude, he pointedly contrasts TV coverage of elections with the old days—like the time a politician brought a white bear to a rally and it spooked young Ariah's horse.

Ed's comparison of a bear with TV brings the novel full circle. When Sally came to live with him, James told her ''that if she wanted TV she could watch it in the shed. . . . God made the world to be looked at head on, and let a bear live in the woodshed, he'd soon have your bed'' (4). When Richard had killed himself, James had prowled the countryside ''like a lost bear hunting for the door to the underworld . . .'' (303). And when James finally discovers that Richard did not kill himself out of a perverse vengeance against him, ''it was as if, suddenly, he had fallen back into the world, found the magic door'' (427).

Gardner resolves the metaphor of the bear by giving it flesh. When James thinks of Ariah and the bear, his emotions begin to unlock (like Vermont in the spring). Later, while wintering his beehives, and lost in memories of Ariah, he has his own experience with a bear, beginning with "a smell of wildness" (433). It is the smell associated with Uncle Ira's coat—and with Richard, who wore the coat and scared Horace into a heart attack. But it is also the smell that frightened Ariah's horse and now frightens the "lost bear," James, who scared Ruth's "bear" into a heart attack. When James turns around he sees an enormous black bear standing five feet away from him—an aged bear, a mirror of himself, the symbolic aggregate of all the witless bears (and humans) that prowl James's world.

Fortunately James does not shoot the bear. To shoot the bear would be to repeat the crime of shooting the witless TV—his metaphorical albatross—and to again destroy his spiritual connectedness with life. When James fired at the TV set, Sally had "shot up three feet into the air . . ." (4); when James—governed by "something" that jerks the gun—fires at the sky, the "bear jumped three feet into the air and began shaking exactly as the old man was doing . . ." (434). In paralleling the bear's cartoon reaction to Sally's cartoon reaction, and in paralleling the bear's "shaking" to James's shaking, Gardner creates an ironic, if not a grotesque, portrait of spiritual unity and connectedness, while parodying Faulkner's "The Bear." In developing his parody of Faulkner's novella and its theme of connectedness, Gardner has Lewis Hicks echo the question put to Faulkner's protagonist, Isaac McCaslin, by his cousin, McCaslin Edmonds: " 'And you didn't shoot at him?' Lewis said, looking thoughtfully past him with that one blue eye, one brown eye" (434). But like Isaac McCaslin, James does not know why he did not shoot at the bear, who had, like Lewis, "something not quite right about the eyes" (433); he only knows that the bear seemed to say to him, echoing Ariah, "distinctly, reproachfully, *Oh James, James!*"

By juxtaposing Lewis with his mismatched eyes and a bear with strange eyes who seemingly talks like Ariah, and by counterpointing a scene from Faulkner's "The Bear" in *October Light* with a scene from TV's "Star Trek" in *The Smugglers of Lost Souls' Rock,* Gardner widens the irony of his climactic scene, and thus the distance between the reader and the potential sentimentality of James's emotional redemption.

October Light is extravagantly metafictional. Gardner continually breaks the "vivid and continuous dream," calling attention to the competing texts and emphasizing the counterpoint between the fictive worlds with the radically different illustrations by Raphael and Bolognese: realistically detailed pen and ink drawings for *October Light* itself, but expressionistic line and wash drawings for *The Smugglers.* Though Gardner had misgivings about his disruption of the narratives, he could see no other way to dramatize the impact of fiction on a character. Henry James—an early influence on Gardner's work—spoke, in his preface to *The Portrait of a Lady,* of the many "windows" in the "House of Fiction." James wanted his readers to see clearly—without distraction—through the windows of the text into the fictive "life" he had created. By contrast, Gardner's disrupted texts remind his readers of the windows through which they are seeing the fiction, and the windows mediate the fictive experience, inducing a continual comparison, hinting at incongruities and suggesting ironies. In making the reader conscious of the page, however, Gardner created the kind of textual "opacity" (69) that he later condemned in *On Moral Fiction.*

When Gardner wrote "The King's Indian," he still apparently believed, as he told Joe David Bellamy, that writers should create stories that are "moment-by-moment wonderful, which are true to human experience, and which in no way explain human experience," and that "wonderful sand castles are terrific; I think they're moral. I think they make you a better person much more than a sermon does."[11] When he wrote *On Moral Fiction,* however, he used the same "sand castle" metaphor to condemn the kind of fiction he had once written himself and praised:

> . . . our writers concentrate, to a greater or lesser extent, on language for its own sake, more in love, on principle, with the sound of words—or with new fangledness—than with creating fictional worlds. One might say, in their defense, that what they create is "linguistic sculpture." . . . But the fact remains that their search for opacity has little to do with the age-old search for understanding and affirmation. Linguistic sculpture at best makes only the affirmation sandcastles make, that it is pleasant to make things or look at things made, better to be alive than dead. (71)

Since Gardner apparently wrote these comments about textual "opacity" shortly after completing *October Light,*[12] they may partially reflect his ultimate dissatisfaction with the novel's structure. During this same period, he told Roni Natov and Geraldine DeLuca that the "tale within a tale" of *October Light* was counterproductive: "Every time you shift from one gear to another, the reader says, 'No, I don't want to read that trash novel now.' "[13]

But despite Gardner's misgivings, *October Light* was a critical as well as a commercial success. Though not all readers liked the disrupted narrative, many found it intriguing and entertaining, and even those who disliked the interruptions tolerated them because they found the characters of James and Sally so compelling. Indeed, this diversity of response was typified by the select committee for the National Book Critics Circle Award, when it awarded the prize to Gardner by a majority of one vote. Digby Diehl expressed no such reservations, however, when he presented the award. He had saluted *Grendel* with enthusiasm on 5 September 1971, and he saluted *October Light* with even more enthusiasm on 13 January 1977, calling it

> a marvelously entertaining, happily readable book, which surrounds its moments of profundity with fun, even zaniness. For all the sprawling breadth of its themes, this novel has prose that crackles with energy. It is a virtuoso work of lyric flights, jazzy excitements, and absorbing meditations. Most strikingly, *October Light* is a deeply American book. From the wisps of Robert Frost in his descriptions of New England to the rock-and-roll jangle of his pop culture scenes, Gardner hears this country singing in a clear and coherent way that is in center stream of our national literary tradition. With this, his eighth book and most stunning achievement, we celebrate the emergence of a major American novelist, John Gardner.[14]

Regrettably, however, though Gardner continued to publish at a furious rate, he was unable to achieve either the critical or popular success of *October Light*—not to mention *The Sunlight Dialogues* or *Grendel*—and five years later he was dead.

NOTES

1. John Gardner, *October Light* (New York: Knopf, 1976) 3–4. Parenthetical page references in the text are to this edition.

2. Gardner anticipates James Page's hostility toward the commercialization of the Bicentennial in ''Amber (Get) Waves (Your) of (Plastic) Grain (Uncle Sam),'' *New York Times* 29 Oct. 1975: 41; see Gregory L. Morris, *A World of Order and Light: The Fiction of John Gardner* (Athens: University of Georgia Press, 1984) 143–45.

Understanding John Gardner

3. See Robert A. Morace, "New Fiction, Popular Fiction, and John Gardner's Middle/Moral Way," *John Gardner: Critical Perspectives,* ed. Robert A. Morace and Kathryn VanSpanckeren (Carbondale: Southern Illinois University Press, 1982) 138–45.

4. For a more detailed discussion of these and other allusions, see David Cowart, *Arches and Light: The Fiction of John Gardner* (Carbondale: Southern Illinois University Press, 1983) 114–21.

5. See also Cowart 117–20.

6. Roni Natov and Geraldine DeLuca, "An Interview with John Gardner," *The Lion and the Unicorn* 2 (Spring 1978): 125.

7. John Gardner, *The Art of Fiction: Notes on Craft for Young Writers* (New York: Knopf, 1984) 47. Parenthetical page references in the text are to this edition.

8. John Gardner, *On Moral Fiction* (New York: Basic Books, 1978) 36. Parenthetical page references in the text are to this edition.

9. See Leonard Butts's discussion of "saintly intercessors," in *The Novels of John Gardner: Making Life Art as a Moral Process* (Baton Rouge: Louisiana State University Press, 1988) 45–46 *passim.*

10. John Gardner, *The Sunlight Dialogues* (New York: Knopf, 1972) 620.

11. Joe David Bellamy and Pat Ensworth, "John Gardner," *The New Fiction: Interviews with Innovative American Writers,* ed. Joe David Bellamy (Urbana: University of Illinois Press, 1974) 180, 191.

12. Though Gardner apparently drafted the first six chapters of *On Moral Fiction* in early 1976, allusions in the typescript (to contemporary publications) suggest that he drafted the last three chapters in 1967.

13. Natov and DeLuca 131.

14. Digby Diehl, "Transcript of Awards Ceremony," *The National Book Critics Circle Journal* 3 (Spring 1977): 3.

CHAPTER SEVEN

Other Works

John Gardner was as versatile as he was prolific. His literary reputation is based on his fiction, particularly his novels. But he also wrote an epic, a biography, critical and scholarly studies, verse translations of epics and medieval romances, and comic fantasies for children—notably, *Dragon, Dragon and Other Tales,* chosen as *"The New York Times* Outstanding Book for Children in 1975," and offered by Book-of-the-Month Club in a three-volume set with *Gudgekin the Thistle Girl and Other Tales* (1976) and *The King of the Hummingbirds and Other Tales* (1977).

Gardner combined his love of fantasy with his love of music and theater. He had played French horn and written musicals as a college student. In the 1970s he wrote (and published) three opera librettos: *Frankenstein* (1979); *William Wilson* (1979); and *Rumpelstiltskin* (1978), an opera for children produced by the Philadelphia Opera Company. And he also wrote radio plays—his play *The Temptation Game* won the Armstrong Prize for its performance on NPR's *Earplay* and was published by Gardner in 1980.

Ultimately, however, Gardner saw his explorations in other media as "vacations" from the central purpose of his career—the writing of novels and tales. And to fully appreciate Gardner's achievement as a writer of fiction, the reader should have at least a cursory awareness of Gardner's other efforts in this genre.

The Wreckage of Agathon

Though *The Wreckage of Agathon* (1970) is not one of Gardner's major works, it is not, as his widely read comment in *The New Fiction* suggests, a "terrible book."[1] It is in fact, as Robert Wernick observed in *Time* magazine, "a sharp and provoking little antihistorical novel."[2] Gardner borrows extensively and whimsically from John Dryden's translation of *Plutarch's Lives of the Noble Grecians and Romans,* while echoing the ideas of Sartre, Plato, and Whitehead.[3] And he introduces numerous anachronisms, setting the novel between 600 and 560 B.C., supposedly during the reign of Lykourgos (who perhaps existed around 900 B.C.) in Sparta, and of Solon in Athens; and featuring Agathon, partially inspired by the poet Agathon (448 B.C.–402 B.C.), mentioned in both Plato's *Symposium* and Aristotle's *Poetics.*

In Gardner's novel, Agathon is not only an Athenian poet, but also a "seer," philosopher, and Solon's scribe. When he goes to Sparta to serve Lykourgos, however, he taunts him once too often, and is thrown into a prison cell, where he carries on a dialogue (and narrates alternate chapters) with his young disciple, Demodokos (nicknamed "Peeker"). Like Taggert Hodge (whom he echoes) and Grendel (whom he anticipates), Agathon is comically grotesque and filled with despair. Ultimately, Peeker is the novel's artist-hero, who survives to complete the story of Agathon's last days.

Jason and Medeia

Though Gardner dismissed *The Wreckage of Agathon* as a failure, he continued to defend *Jason and Medeia* (1973). Inspired by the success of *Grendel,* with its parody of the Anglo-Saxon epic *Beowulf,* Gardner responded to a Greek epic. But unlike *Grendel, Jason and Medeia* closely parallels the structure of its source—Apollonius of Rhodes's *Argonautica,* a minor epic written in Alexandria (c. 350) and featuring Jason's voyage on the *Argo.* Employing a self-consciously modern and, finally, intrusive narrator (as in "The King's Indian"), Gardner focuses on Jason's conflict with Medeia, drawing on Euripides' *Medea* (451 B.C.) to objectify the heroine's passionate conflict with the coldly rationalistic—ultimately nihilistic—Jason. And to create the poetic rhythm of the narrative, Gardner converts the Greek hexameter lines of the original epic into what he called "sprung hexameters," a form (inspired by Richard Lattimore's translations of Homer) which establishes and plays against a six-beat line but almost continuously varies the stress.[4] In the end, however, Gardner's recapitulation of the text of the *Argonautica* was perhaps more of a burden than an inspiration. Though *Jason and Medeia* has many brilliant moments, it taxed Gardner's poetic gifts and often turned him to prose. Indeed, *Jason and Medeia* probably succeeds more as a "novel," as one reviewer called it, than an epic poem.

Freddy's Book

Reviewers were even more uncertain about what to call *Freddy's Book* (1980). The work consists of two novellas—"Freddy" and "Freddy's Book"—and their relationship is not immediately clear. "Freddy" is narrated by Professor Jack Winesap, who meets Professor Sven Agaard after giving a paper on "The Psycho-politics of the Late Welsh Fairytale: Fee,

Fie, Foe—Revolution!'' Professor Agaard disdains Winesap's psychohistorical explication of ''Jack and the Beanstalk'' and the giant (''Fee, Fie, Foe [Fum]''). But Agaard's reclusive son, Freddy—a giant himself—is a fan of Winesap's scholarship, and Agaard invites Winesap home to meet him. Though Winesap discovers that Freddy is indeed, as his father bluntly says, a ''monster,'' he also discovers that Freddy is intelligent as well as pathetic—and he impulsively gives him the paper he has just read. During the night Freddy reciprocates by leaving his ''book'' on the floor of Winesap's bedroom.

As Gardner presents him, Freddy is a novice trying to write a metaphysical tale (''King Gustav & the Devil''), and he begins by echoing, almost verbatim and in a relatively wooden style, two books from his father's library.[5] However, as he gets caught up in the metaphysical adventures of his hero, Lars-Goren Bergquist, a sixteenth-century Swedish knight, his style becomes more supple.[6] Lars-Goren, whom Freddy projects as a giant, has helped King Gustav Vasa beat the Danes. But the Devil also helped, and when the Devil continues to create chaos, the king asks Lars-Goren (an idealist) and Bishop Hans Brask (a nihilist) to destroy him. On their journey to mystical ''Lappland,'' where the Devil is resting on a mountaintop, the two antithetical thinkers engage in a metaphysical debate familiar to readers of Gardner's earlier works.

The dust jacket blurb for *Freddy's Book* confuses readers by describing the title novella as ''an irresistible novel within a novel, a metaphysical folktale.'' But the ''novel''—or ''tale''—is not, technically, within the narrative of ''Freddy,'' since Gardner never returns to the original narrative. Apparently, Gardner felt it was unnecessary: the dust jacket claims that Freddy's tale ''poignantly mirrors the young man's own secret anguish and fantasy, his moving and troubled relationship with his father.'' But many readers failed to appreciate either how Freddy's emotional projection mirrors his concerns, or how the initially awkward style of the ''book'' reflects his naivete as a teller of tales. And many were frustrated by Gardner's failure to complete the frame promised by the opening novella. However, though *Freddy's Book* received a generally lukewarm response, the fantasy writer Ursula LeGuin called it ''a brilliant novel,''[7] and it may yet find the audience that Gardner envisioned.

The Art of Living and Other Stories

The Art of Living and Other Stories (1981) elicited even more contradictory responses. In spring 1975, Gardner drafted, then abandoned, the intensely autobiographical novel ''Stillness,'' which focused on the lives of novelist/professor Martin Orrick, called ''Buddy'' (Gardner's own nickname), and his wife Joan, who live in southern Missouri (cf. southern Illinois). However, before abandoning the novel (published posthumously, in 1986, with the unfinished novel ''Shadows'')[8] Gardner extracted and published two short stories—''Redemption'' and ''Stillness''—later collecting them with ''Nimram,'' ''The Music Lover,'' ''Trumpeter,'' ''The Library Horror,'' ''The Joy of the Just,'' ''Vlemk the Box-Painter,'' ''Come on Back,'' and the title story, ''The Art of Living.''

Though all the stories but ''The Art of Living'' were published separately over a period of seven years (1974–1981), there is a remarkable continuity of theme: all but two of them (''The Library Horror'' and ''The Joy of the Just'') resolve their conflicts by affirming, either directly or implicitly, the redemptive power of art. At the time the book was published, some reviewers—influenced by *On Moral Fiction* (1978)—maintained that Gardner was enslaved by his own manifesto; that he was imposing the theme of artistic redemption on his characters. Though this is perhaps an exaggerated response to Gardner's thematic concerns, most readers now seem to agree that the three autobiographical fictions in *The Art of Living* ("Come on Back," "Redemption," and "Stillness") are the most compelling, because they are less programmatic and more deeply felt. In "Come on Back," Gardner's persona remembers the Welsh choral festival "Cmanfa Ganu" ("Come on Back" [to Wales]); the death (by suicide) of his "Uncle Charley," once a great singer; and the transcendent singing on the night after Uncle Charley's death. In "Redemption," Gardner's persona remembers the trauma and guilt of accidentally killing his little brother; the escape into the abstract world of French horn music; and the paradoxical redemption which came with the recognition that he had a limited talent. In "Stillness," Gardner's first wife Joan looks back from middle age and sees herself as a teenager playing piano accompaniment at The Duggers School of the Dance, and remembers the magic of Pete Duggers's tap routine which built to a crescendo of shuffles and turns—and ended, transcendentally, with "a sudden stillness like an escape from reality. . . ."

Less subtle in its artistic affirmation, "Nimram" tells the story of a world-famous symphony conductor, Benjamin Nimram, who befriends a dying girl on a plane to Chicago, where he conducts the Chicago Symphony in a rousing performance of Mahler's Fifth, momentarily transporting the girl out of time—and death. Thematically related in its affirmation—but ironically antithetical in approach—"The Music Lover" borrows from Thomas Mann's "Disillusionment" to describe how an aging professor, with a deep but naive love of orchestral music, suffers through a performance of postmodernist music—only to be buttonholed and harangued by its nihilistic and angry composer.

Also concerned with art—but fantastic rather than realistic in presentation—are "Trumpeter," the original resolution of the Queen Louisa tales in *The King's Indian;* and "Vlemk the Box-Painter," a novella that Gardner originally published alone in a collectors' edition. Trumpeter—a dog—naively reports what he sees, failing to understand either the implications of Princess Muriel's terminal illness or mad Queen Louisa's transformation of her kingdom into a work of art. Vlemk—a brilliant artist—paints a talking portrait of an egocentric princess on a box, including all her imperfections, but then effects her redemption by removing them (in a prolix, though generally entertaining, allegory). More successful—though its ending was too grotesque for some readers—is the climactic story, "The Art of Living," in which chef Arnold Deller prepares an exotic dish of "Imperial Dog" in memory of his son Rinehart, who had written with reverence about the ancient dish shortly before his death in the Vietnam War.[9]

Mickelsson's Ghosts

Gardner's sense of an ending also disturbed reviewers of *Mickelsson's Ghosts* (1982), the last novel published during his lifetime—and second only to *The Sunlight Dialogues* in length. Conceived as a Gothic "potboiler" to pay off his crippling debt to the Internal Revenue Service, *Mickelsson's Ghosts* went through a troubled gestation. Though Gardner began by introducing familiar Gothic elements—a half-mad hero, a beautiful woman in distress, a haunted house, and ostensibly supernatural murders—the novel gradually modulated, like his earlier works, toward a philosophical debate between faith (personified by Martin Luther's ideas—and ghost) and doubt (personified by Friedrich Nietzsche's ideas—and ghost), while building more and more on the details of Gardner's troubled life.

Formerly a professor of philosophy at Brown University and a highly respected scholar, Mickelsson is in the middle of an emotional breakdown when he comes to the State University of New York at Binghamton. There, like Gardner, he has problems with the IRS and his ex-wife, and misses his two children. Desperately trying to regain control over his life and emotions, Mickelsson buys a farmhouse near Susquehanna, Pennsylvania, some thirty miles away from Binghamton. But instead of finding an idyll, he immediately discovers ghosts, including the house's former tenants and the philosophical antagonists Luther and Nietzsche.

Though *Mickelsson's Ghosts* contains some of Gardner's best writing and characters, the murder plot fails to mesh and energize its narrative strands and metaphysical concerns. As reviewers observed, the weakness of the murder plot is especially evident when Mickelsson has his obligatory confrontation with the killer. Since the killer's motivation is unconvincing, the scene seems arbitrary and imposed, and it highlights the plot's failure. But almost as disturbing to some readers is the novel's final scene. Here, Mickelsson—dressed like a clown, his face white with plaster dust—moves suddenly from murders, hallucinations, and the madness of despair to a grotesquely comical action in which he affirms his humanity by protesting his love for, and copulating with, Jessica Stark on a bed surrounded by the ghosts of people and animals, some smiling obscenely, others covering their eyes.

In developing this scene Gardner is parodying the actions of James Chandler in *The Resurrection*, whose spirit haunts Mickelsson's character more systematically than any of the ghosts in the novel. Like Chandler, Mickelsson is a professor of philosophy who suffers an emotional breakdown, who objectifies his madness by projecting the ghost of an old woman, who carries on a metaphysical debate in his mind but fails to write, who becomes infatuated with a reckless teenage girl, and who parodies the moment when Nietzsche prostrated himself at Cosima Wagner's feet—and found the "amazing grace" that he had eliminated from his philosophical system.[10] But Chandler's moment of grace was simply the last burst of consciousness at the time of his death; Mickelsson's moment of grace has the ambiguous promise of a future. Gardner had parodied *The Rime of the Ancient Mariner* in ending *The Sunlight Dialogues, Grendel,* "The King's Indian," and *October Light.* He does so again in *Mickelsson's Ghosts.* At the beginning of the novel, Mickelsson falls from grace when he is confronted by a "black Doberman, or perhaps a Great Dane," and, "quick as a snake" (8), he kills it with his walking stick. At the end of the novel, Mickelsson moves toward grace when he is confronted by a friendly dog, a "golden Lab," which seems about to talk, and he says to himself, "happy the snake, eggs indifferently buried in the earth and forsaken!" (583), Gardner's final, ironic salute to Coleridge's water snakes.

Although some students of Gardner's fiction rank *Mickelsson's Ghosts* as one of his "major" novels, they do so largely on the basis of its great potential rather than on its achievement. To do so, however, is to blur the achievement of *Grendel, The Sunlight Dialogues,* and *October Light,* which was great indeed.

Understanding John Gardner

NOTES

1. Joe David Bellamy and Pat Ensworth, "John Gardner," *The New Fiction: Interviews with Innovative American Writers,* ed. Joe David Bellamy (Urbana: University of Illinois Press, 1974) 190.

2. Robert Wernick, "Seer v. Slob," *Time* 9 Nov. 1970: 86.

3. For a detailed discussion of Gardner's sources for this novel, see Gregory L. Morris, *A World of Order and Light: The Fiction of John Gardner* (Athens: University of Georgia Press, 1984) 38–50, 232–34.

4. For Gardner's definition of "sprung hexameters," see Charlie Reilly, "A Conversation with John Gardner," *Classical and Modern Literature* 1 (Winter 1981): 105–6.

5. Gregory L. Morris identifies the two books that Freddy borrows from as Ingvar Andersson's *A History of Sweden* and Michael Roberts's *The Early Vasas: A History of Sweden, 1523–1611;* see Morris 168.

6. See Robert A. Morace's analysis of Freddy's stylistic growth, in "*Freddy's Book,* Moral Fiction, and Writing as a Mode of Thought," *Modern Fiction Studies* 29 (Summer 1983): 201–12.

7. See Ursula LeGuin, "Where Giants Roam," *Washington Post Book World* 23 Mar.1980: 1.

8. Knopf published "Stillness," along with fragments of the unfinished novel "Shadows," four years after Gardner's death; see John Gardner, *"Stillness" and "Shadows",* ed. Nicholas Delbanco (New York: Knopf, 1986).

9. For a detailed examination of these stories, as well as "The Library Horror" and "The Joy of the Just," see Jeff Henderson, *John Gardner: A Study of the Short Fiction* (Boston: Twayne, 1990) 62–89.

10. John Gardner, *Mickelsson's Ghosts* (New York: Knopf, 1982) 578. Parenthetical page references in the text are to this edition.

Works by John Gardner
Novels
The Resurrection. New York: New American Library, 1966. Rev. ed. New York: Ballantine, 1974.

The Wreckage of Agathon. New York: Harper & Row, 1970.

Grendel. Illus. Emil Antonucci. New York: Knopf, 1971. London: Deutsch, 1972.

The Sunlight Dialogues. Illus. John Napper. New York: Knopf, 1972. London: Cape, 1973.

Nickel Mountain: A Pastoral Novel. Illus. Thomas O'Donohue. New York: Knopf, 1973. London: Cape, 1974.

October Light. Illus. Elaine Raphael and Don Bolognese. New York: Knopf, 1976. London: Cape, 1977.

Freddy's Book. Illus. Daniel Biamonte. New York: Knopf, 1980. London: Secker & Warburg, 1981.

Mickelsson's Ghosts. Illus. Joel Gardner. New York: Knopf, 1982. London: Secker & Warburg, 1983.

"Stillness" and "Shadows". Ed. with intro. Nicholas Delbanco. New York: Knopf, 1986.

Unpublished Novel
"The Old Men." Diss. State University of Iowa. 1958. [Ann Arbor: University Microfilms, 1959.]

Short Fiction
The King's Indian: Stories and Tales. Illus. Herbert L. Fink. New York: Knopf, 1974. London: Cape, 1975.

The Art of Living and Other Stories. Illus. Mary Azarian. New York: Knopf, 1981.

Poetry
Jason and Medeia. New York: Knopf, 1973.

Poems. Northridge, CA: Lord John Press, 1978.

Biography

The Life & Times of Chaucer. Illus. J. Wolf. New York: Knopf, 1977. London: Cape, 1977.

Children's Books

Dragon, Dragon and Other Tales. Illus. Charles Shields. New York: Knopf, 1975.

Gudgekin the Thistle Girl and Other Tales. Illus. Michael Sporn. New York: Knopf, 1976.

The King of the Hummingbirds and Other Tales. Illus. Michael Sporn. New York: Knopf, 1977.

A Child's Bestiary. Illus. Gardner et al. New York: Knopf, 1977.

In the Suicide Mountains. Illus. Joe Servello. New York: Knopf, 1977.

Radio Plays

The Temptation Game. Dallas: New London Press, 1980.

Death and the Maiden. Dallas: New London Press, 1981.

Opera Libretti

Rumpelstiltskin. Dallas: New London Press, 1978.

Frankenstein. Dallas: New London Press, 1979.

William Wilson. Dallas: New London Press, 1979.

Translations

The Complete Works of the Gawain-Poet in a Modern English Version with a Critical Introduction by John Gardner. Illus. Fritz Kredel. Chicago: University of Chicago Press, 1965.

The Alliterative Morte Arthure The Owl and the Nightingale And Five Other Middle English Poems in a Modernized Version with Comments on the Poems and Notes by John Gardner. Carbondale: Southern Illinois University Press, 1971.

Tengu Child: Stories by Kikuo Itaya. Ed. and trans. with Nobuko Tsukui. Carbondale: Southern Illinois University Press, 1983.

Gilgamesh. Ed. and trans. with John Maier. New York: Knopf, 1984.

Bibliography

Literary Criticism

Le Morte Darthur Notes. Lincoln, Nebr.: Cliff's Notes, 1967.

The Gawain-Poet Notes. Lincoln, Nebr.: Cliff's Notes, 1967.

The Construction of the Wakefield Cycle. Carbondale: Southern Illinois University Press, 1974.

The Construction of Christian Poetry in Old English. Carbondale: Southern Illinois University Press, 1975.

The Poetry of Chaucer. Carbondale: Southern Illinois University Press, 1977.

On Moral Fiction. New York: Basic Books, 1978.

On Becoming a Novelist. Foreword by Raymond Carver. New York: Harper & Row, 1983.

The Art of Fiction: Notes on Craft for Young Writers. New York: Knopf, 1984.

Selected Uncollected Essays

"Fulgentius's *Expositio Vergiliana Continentia* and the Plan of *Beowulf:* Another Approach to the Poem's Style and Structure." *Papers on Language and Literature* 6 (Summer 1970): 227–62.

"The Way We Write Now." *New York Times Book Review* 9 July 1972: 2, 32–33.

"Saint Walt [Disney]: The Greatest Artist the World Has Ever Known, Except for Possibly Apollonius of Rhodes." *New York* 12 Nov. 1973: 64–71.

"Amber (Get) Waves (Your) of (Plastic) Grain (Uncle Sam)." *New York Times* 29 Oct. 1975: 41.

"A Writer's View of Contemporary American Fiction." *Dismisura* [Altari, Italy] 39–50 (Dec. 1980): 11–31.

"What Writers Do." *Antaeus* 40–41 (Winter-Spring 1981): 416–26.

"Learning from Disney and Dickens." *New York Times Book Review* 30 Jan. 1983: 3, 22–23. Rpt. as "Cartoons." *In Praise of What Persists.* Ed. Stephen Berg. New York: Harper & Row, 1983. 125–34.

Bibliography

Works Edited by Gardner

MSS 1 (1961), 1 (1962), and 2 (1964), ed. Gardner et al.; *MSS* 1–3 (1981–1984), ed. Gardner and L. M. Rosenberg.

The Forms of Fiction. Ed. Gardner and Lennis Dunlap. New York: Random House, 1962.

The Construction of "Paradise Lost." By Burton Jasper Weber. Ed. with foreword by Gardner. Carbondale: Southern Illinois University Press, 1971.

Forms of Glory: Structure and Sense in Virgil's "Aeneid." By J. William Hunt. Ed. with foreword by Gardner. Carbondale: Southern Illinois University Press, 1973.

Wedges and Wings: The Patterning of "Paradise Regained." By Burton Jasper Weber. Ed. with foreword by Gardner. Carbondale: Southern Illinois University Press, 1974.

Music from Home: Selected Poems. By Colleen J. McElroy. Ed. with preface by Gardner. Carbondale: Southern Illinois University Press, 1976.

Homer's "Iliad": The Shield of Memory. By Kenneth John Atchity. Ed. with foreword by Gardner. Carbondale: Southern Illinois University Press, 1978.

Kingship and Common Profit in Gower's "Confessio Amantis." By Russell A. Peck. Ed. with foreword by Gardner. Carbondale: Southern Illinois University Press, 1978.

Flamboyant Drama: A Study of "The Castle of Perseverance," "Mankind," and "Wisdom." By Michael R. Kelley. Ed. with foreword by Gardner. Carbondale: Southern Illinois University Press, 1979.

Epic and Romance in the Argonautica of Apollonius. By Charles Rowan Beye. Ed. with foreword by Gardner. Carbondale: Southern Illinois University Press, 1982.

The Best American Short Stories. Ed. Gardner and Shannon Ravenel. Boston: Houghton Mifflin, 1982.

Selected Interviews

Books

Chavkin, Allan, ed. *Conversations with John Gardner.* Jackson: University Press of Mississippi, 1990.

Renwick, Joyce, and Howard Smith. *John Gardner: An Interview.* Dallas: New London Press, 1980.

Book Sections and Articles

Allen, Henry. "John Gardner: 'I'm One of the Really Great Writers.' " *Washington Post Magazine* 6 Nov. 1977: 23, 28, 33, 37.

Beans, Bruce. "John Gardner's Last Interview." *Today:* [Philadelphia] *Inquirer Magazine* 17 Oct. 1982: 1, 18–21.

Burns, Alan. "John Gardner." *The Imagination on Trial: British and American Writers Discuss Their Working Methods.* Ed. Alan Burns and Charles Sugnet. London: Allison and Busby, 1981. 40–50.

Christian, Ed. "An Interview with John Gardner." *Prairie Schooner* 54 (Winter 1980–1981): 70–93.

Clark, C. E. Frazer, Jr. "John Gardner." *Conversations with Writers.* Vol 1. Detroit: Bruccoli Clark/Gale, 1977. 83–103.

Cuomo, Joseph, and Marie Ponsot. "An Interview with John Gardner." *A Shout in the Street* 1.2 (1977): 45–63.

Diehl, Digby. "Medievalist in Illinois Ozarks." *Los Angeles Times* 5 Sept. 1971: 43.

Edwards, Don, and Carol Polsgrove. "A Conversation with John Gardner." *Atlantic* 239 (May 1977): 43–47.

Bellamy, Joe David, and Pat Ensworth. "John Gardner: An Interview." *The New Fiction: Interviews with Innovative American Writers.* Ed. Joe David Bellamy. Urbana: University of Illinois Press, 1974. 169–93.

Ferguson, Paul F., John R. Maier, Frank McConnell, and Sara Matthiessen. "The Art of Fiction LXXIII: John Gardner." *Paris Review* 21 (Spring 1979): 36–74. Rpt. in *Writers at Work, Sixth Series.* Ed. George Plimpton. New York: Viking, 1984.

Bibliography

Harvey, Marshall L. "Where Philosophy and Fiction Meet: An Interview with John Gardner." *Chicago Review* 29 (1978): 73–87.

"John Gardner: A Defense Against Darkness." Prod. and dir. Richard O. Moore. *The Originals: The Writer in America.* PBS, 3 April 1978. [Produced in 1975 by Perspective Films, 369 West Erie Street, Chicago, Ill. 60610.]

Laskin, Daniel. "Challenging the Literary Naysayers." *Horizon* 21 (July 1978): 32–36.

LeClair, Thomas. "William Gass and John Gardner: A Debate On Fiction." *New Republic* 10 Mar. 1979: 25, 28–33.

Members of the English Department, Pan American University. "Interview with John Gardner." *John Gardner: True Art, Moral Art.* Ed. Beatrice Mendez-Egle. Edinburg, Tex.: Pan American University School of Humanities, 1983. 96–111.

Mitcham, Judson, and William Richard. "An Interview with John Gardner." *New Orleans Review* 8 (Summer 1981): 124–33.

Natale, Richard. "John Gardner: 'Great Age of the Novel Is Returning.' " *Women's Wear Daily* 8 Dec. 1972: 16.

Natov, Roni, and Geraldine DeLuca. "An Interview with John Gardner." *The Lion and the Unicorn* 2 (Spring 1978): 114–36.

Reilly, Charlie. "A Conversation with John Gardner." *Classical and Modern Literature: A Quarterly* 1 (Winter 1981): 91–108.

Singular, Stephen. "The Sound and Fury Over Fiction." *New York Times Magazine* 8 July 1979: 12–15, 34, 36–39.

Suplee, Curt. "John Gardner, Flat Out." *Washington Post* 25 July 1982: H1, H8–H9.

Swindell, Larry. "Our Best Novelist: He Thinks So, Too." *Philadelphia Inquirer* 16 Jan. 1977: F1, F13.

Winther, Per. "An Interview with John Gardner." *English Studies* 62 (Dec. 1981): 509–24.

Ziegler, Heide. "John Gardner." *The Radical Imagination and the Liberal Tradition: Interviews with English and American Authors.* Ed. Heide Ziegler and Christopher Bigsby. London; Junction Books, 1982. 126–50.

Works About John Gardner
Bibliographies

Hamilton, Lee T. "John Gardner: A Bibliographical Update." *John Gardner: True Art, Moral Art.* Ed. Beatrice Mendez-Egle. Edinburg, Tex.: Pan American University School of Humanities, 1983 113–32. Primary and Secondary.

Howell, John M. *John Gardner: A Bibliographical Profile.* Afterword by John Gardner. Carbondale: Southern Illinois University Press, 1980. London: Feffer & Simons, 1980. Primary and Secondary.

Morace, Robert A. *John Gardner: An Annotated Secondary Bibliography.* New York: Garland, 1984.

Books

Butts, Leonard. *The Novels of John Gardner: Making Life Art as a Moral Process.* Baton Rouge: Louisiana State University Press, 1988. Argues that Gardner's protagonists become "moral artists" who search for order and truth, and celebrate existence.

Cowart, David. *Arches and Light: The Fiction of John Gardner.* Carbondale: Southern Illinois University Press, 1983. Analyzes Gardner's ideas, allusions, and techniques in the novels, stories, and children's tales.

Henderson, Jeff. *John Gardner: A Study of the Short Fiction.* Boston: Twayne, 1990. Introduces and analyzes the short fiction, including the children's tales, citing unpublished typescripts and notes, and reprinting excerpts from the work of other critics.

———, ed. *Thor's Hammer: Essays on John Gardner.* Conway: University of Central Arkansas Press, 1985. Includes essays discussing Gardner's apprenticeship, reputation, gothicism, poetry, translations, philosophy, criticism, and themes.

McWilliams, Dean. *John Gardner.* Boston: Twayne, 1990. Employs M. M. Bakhtin's theory of "The Dialogic Imagination" in discussing Gardner's novels, his epic, *Jason and Medeia,* and his "misguided" manifesto, *On Moral Fiction.*

Bibliography

Mendez-Egle, Beatrice, ed. *John Gardner: True Art, Moral Art*. Edinburg, Tex.: Pan American University School of Humanities, 1983. Includes a Gardner interview, an updated primary and secondary bibliography, and critical essays.

Morace, Robert A., and Kathryn VanSpanckeren, eds. *John Gardner: Critical Perspectives*. Afterword by John Gardner. Carbondale: Southern Illinois University Press, 1982. Includes essays treating all aspects of Gardner's literary achievement.

Morris, Gregory L. *A World of Order and Light: The Fiction of John Gardner*. Athens: University of Georgia Press, 1984. Analyzes the sources, forms, and ideas of the fiction, including "The Old Men."

Winther, Per. *The Art of John Gardner: Instruction and Exploration*. Albany: State University of New York Press, 1992. Discusses the philosophical and esthetic sources of *On Moral Fiction* and the ideas and forms of *Grendel, The King's Indian, The Sunlight Dialogues,* and *Jason and Medeia*.

Special Journals

fiction international 12 (1980). Moral Fiction issue. Rpt. *Moral Fiction: An Anthology*. Ed. Joe David Bellamy. Canton, N.Y.: Fiction International, 1980.

MSS 4 (Fall 1984). John Gardner issue.

Articles and Parts of Books

BIOGRAPHICAL

"A Conversation with Priscilla Gardner," with photographs of John Gardner. *MSS* 4 (Fall 1984): 232–49.

Delbanco, Nicholas. "Remembering John Gardner: 'His Moderation Was Our Excess.'" *New York Times Book Review* 11 Nov. 1984: 14–15.

Des Pres, Terrence. "Accident and Its Scene: Reflections on the Death of John Gardner." *Yale Review* 73 (Autumn 1983): 145–60.

Rosenberg, L. M. "John Gardner and *MSS*." *Missouri Review* 7 (Fall 1983): 227–31.

Bibliography

Stansberry, Domenic. "John Gardner: The Return Home." *Plough-shares* 10.2–3 (1984): 95–123.

Williams, Ned. "John Gardner: Letting Go." *Literature and Belief* 2 (1982): 31–36.

CRITICAL

Ackland, Michael. "Blakean Sources in John Gardner's *Grendel.*" *Critique* 23.1 (1981): 57–66. Notes the allusions to Blake's "The Mental Traveller" and *The Marriage of Heaven and Hell,* but suggests that the novel is nihilistic.

Begiebing, Robert J. *Toward a New Synthesis: John Fowles, John Gardner, Norman Mailer.* Ann Arbor, Mich: UMI Research Press, 1989. Discusses the magician-hero of *The Sunlight Dialogues,* who illuminates the gap between human and cosmic orders.

Coale, Samuel Chase. "John Gardner: Slaying the Dragon." *In Hawthorne's Shadow: American Romance from Melville to Mailer.* Lexington: University Press of Kentucky, 1986. 147–60. Explores the Manichean polarities of light and dark, faith and despair, order and chaos.

Ellis, Helen B., and Warren U. Ober. "*Grendel* and Blake: The Contraries of Existence." *English Studies in Canada* 3 (Spring 1977): 87–102. Rpt. Morace and VanSpanckeren, *John Gardner: Critical Perspectives.* Explores Gardner's debt to Blake's idea of contraries, while suggesting the possible influence of monsters created by Shakespeare, Milton, and Browning.

Fawcett, Barry, and Elizabeth Jones. "The Twelve Traps in John Gardner's *Grendel.*" *American Literature* 62 (Dec. 1990): 634–35. Attempts to illustrate Gardner's suggestion that he had tied the main ideas of Western civilization to the twelve sun signs of the zodiac.

Foeller, Elzbieta. "John Gardner's Tale 'The King's Indian' as a Fabulation Based on the 19th-Century Literature Tradition." *Traditions in the Twentieth Century American Literature.* Ed. Marta Sienicka (Poznan, Poland: Adam Mickiewicz University, 1981) 81–89. Explores the major sources of Gardner's parody and the seriousness of his fabulation.

Bibliography

Fredrickson, Robert S. "Losing Battles against Entropy: *The Sunlight Dialogues.*" *Modern Language Studies* 13 (Winter 1983): 47–56. Explores some of the novel's deconstructive aspects and notes how Gardner questions the function of language.

Henderson, Jeff. "The Avenues of Mundane Salvation: Time and Change in the Fiction of John Gardner." *American Literature* 55 (Dec. 1983): 611–33. Illustrates that Gardner's "message . . . is the possibility of mundane salvation, as opposed to the celestial or supernatural, and the principal channels of that salvation are time and change."

———. "John Gardner's *Jason and Medeia:* The Resurrection of a Genre." *Papers on Language and Literature* 22 (Winter 1986): 76–95. Explores the genesis of Gardner's epic, analyzing his use of sources and the development of his themes, characters, and poetry.

Knapp, Peggy A. "Alienated Majesty: *Grendel* and Its Pretexts." *Centennial Review* 32 (Winter 1988): 1–18. Offers a deconstructive reading which argues that Gardner's complex parody of texts leaves the novel's meanings "unresolvable."

Merrill, Robert. "John Gardner's *Grendel* and the Interpretation of Modern Fables." *American Literature* 56 (May 1984): 162–80. Argues that Gardner, like other fabulators, generates sympathy for his misguided narrator (Grendel), leading some readers to mistakenly accept Grendel's nihilistic existentialism as the novel's ultimate signification.

Minugh, David. "John Gardner Constructs *Grendel*'s Universe." *Studies in English Philology, Linguistics, and Literature.* Ed. Mats Rydén and Lennart A. Bjork. Stockholm: Almqvist & Wiksell, 1978. 125–41. Discusses the astrological parallels, noting their philosophical as well as metaphysical implications.

Morace, Robert A. "The Moral Structure of John Gardner's *The King's Indian.*" *Midwest Quarterly* 24 (Summer 1983): 388–99. "Gardner adapts the self-conscious techniques associated with the new fiction to his moral-fiction purposes."

———. "*Freddy's Book,* Moral Fiction, and Writing as a Mode of Thought." *Modern Fiction Studies* 29 (Summer 1983): 201–12. Analyzes Freddy's stylistic growth.

Spraycar, Rudy S. "Mechanism and Medievalism in John Gardner's *Grendel.*" *Science Fiction Dialogues.* Ed. Gary Wolfe. Chicago: Academy Chicago, 1982. 141–52. Explores the relationship between mechanism and Boethian determinism.

Strehle, Susan. "John Gardner's Novels: Affirmation and the Alien." *Critique* 18.2 (1976): 86–96. Observes how Gardner's later works avoid sentimentality and easy affirmation by shifting toward "self-consciousness and humor," and by introducing the nihilistic figure of the "alien."

Stromme, Craig J. "The Twelve Chapters of *Grendel.*" *Critique* 20.1 (1978): 83–92. Discusses the relationship between the astrological signs and the philosophical ideas.

Index

The index does not include reference to material in the notes.

Index

Index

Index

Index

Index